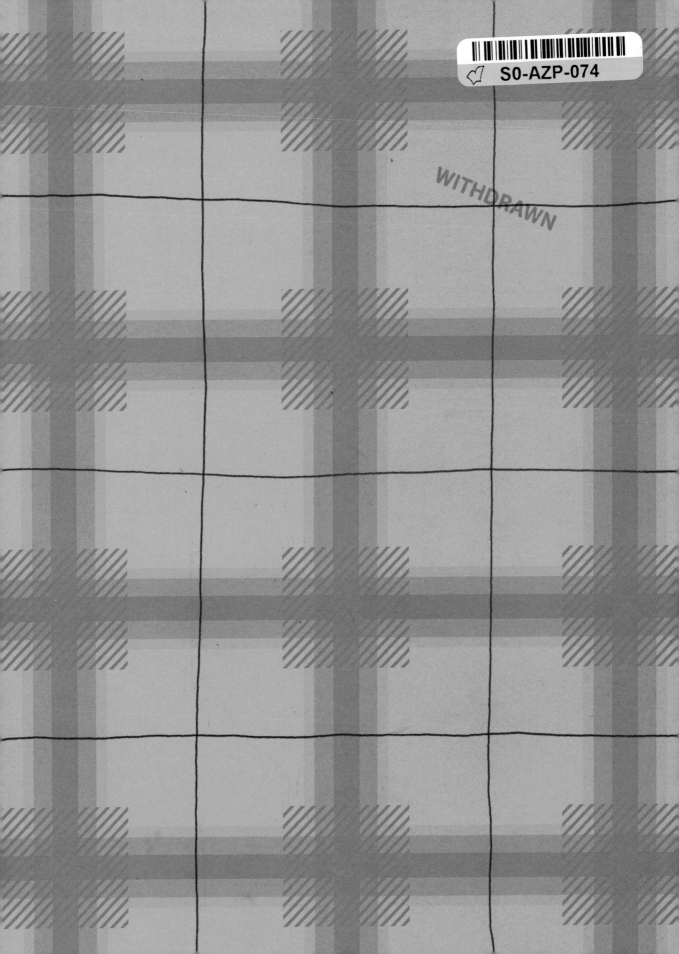

Drawn & Quarterly, Post Office Box 48056, Montreal, Quebec Canada H2V 4S8. *www.drawnandquarterly.com*
First edition: May 2012 • Printed in Thailand • 10   9   8   7   6   5   4   3   2   1
Library and Archives Canada Cataloguing in Publication. Zettwoch, Dan, 1977- Birdseye Bristoe / Dan Zettwoch.
ISBN 978-1-77046-066-9 I. Title. PN6727.Z48B57 2012   741.5'973   C2011-905294-6
Distributed in the USA by: Farrar, Straus and Giroux, 18 West 18th Street, New York, NY 10011 Orders: 888.330.8477
Distributed in Canada by: Raincoast Books 2440 Viking Way Richmond, BC V6V 1N2 Orders: 800.663.5714 Distributed in the
United Kingdom by: Publishers Group UK, 8 The Arena Mollison Avenue, Enfield, Middlesex, EN3 7NL, Orders: 0208.804.0400
ACKNOWLEDGMENTS *The cartoonist thanks Leslie, his family, STL crew, D&Q, Dylan.*

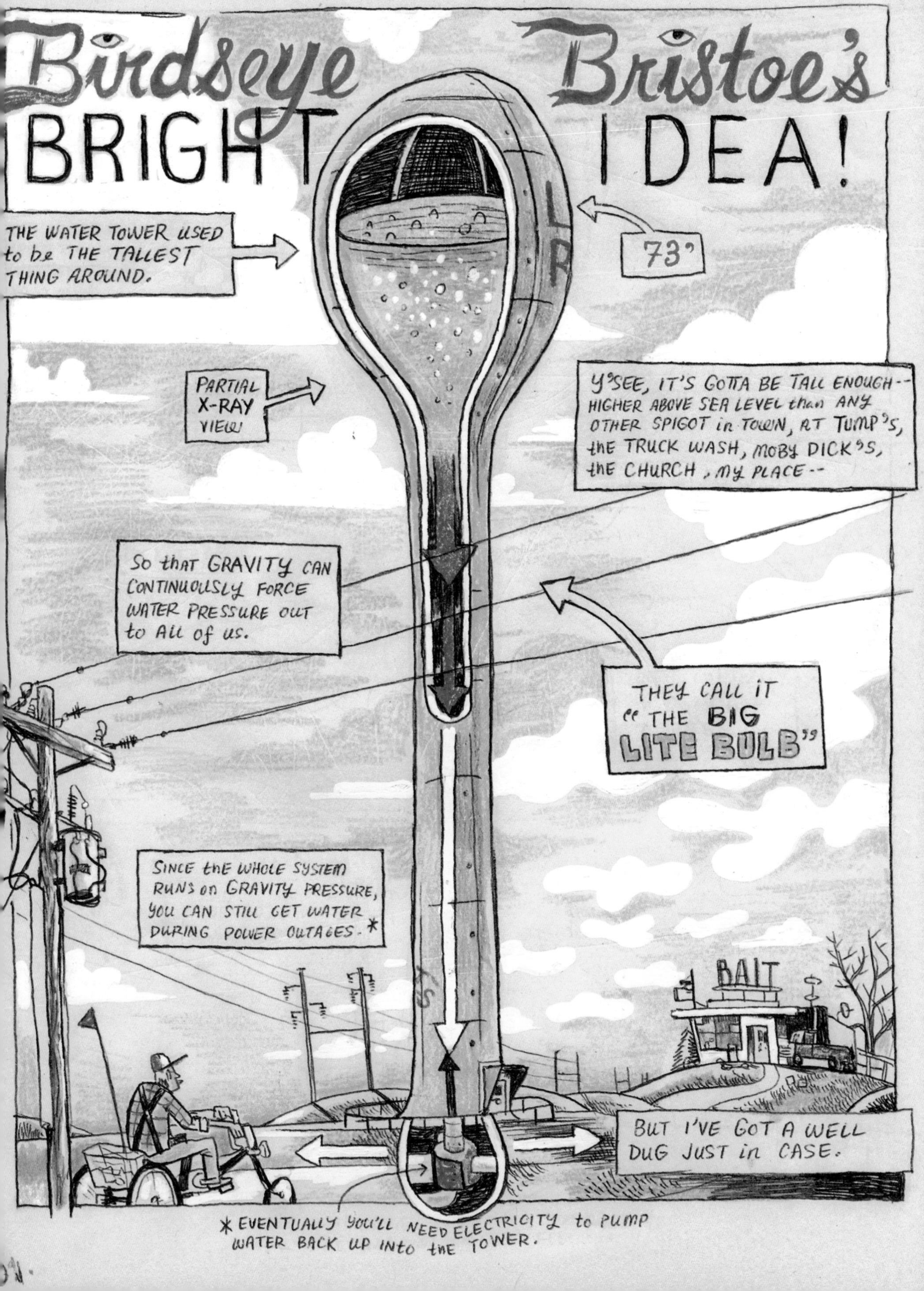

Birdseye Bristoe's
BRIGHT IDEA!
THE WATER TOWER USED to be THE TALLEST THING AROUND.
73°
PARTIAL X-RAY VIEW
Y'SEE, IT'S GOTTA BE TALL ENOUGH-- HIGHER ABOVE SEA LEVEL than ANY OTHER SPIGOT in TOWN, AT TUMP'S, the TRUCK WASH, MOBY DICK'S, the CHURCH, my PLACE--
So that GRAVITY CAN CONTINUOUSLY FORCE WATER PRESSURE OUT to ALL of us.
THEY CALL IT "THE BIG LITE BULB"
SINCE the WHOLE SYSTEM RUNS on GRAVITY PRESSURE, you CAN STILL GET WATER DURING POWER OUTAGES.*
BAIT
BUT I'VE GOT A WELL DUG JUST in CASE.
* EVENTUALLY YOU'LL NEED ELECTRICITY to PUMP WATER BACK UP INTO the TOWER.

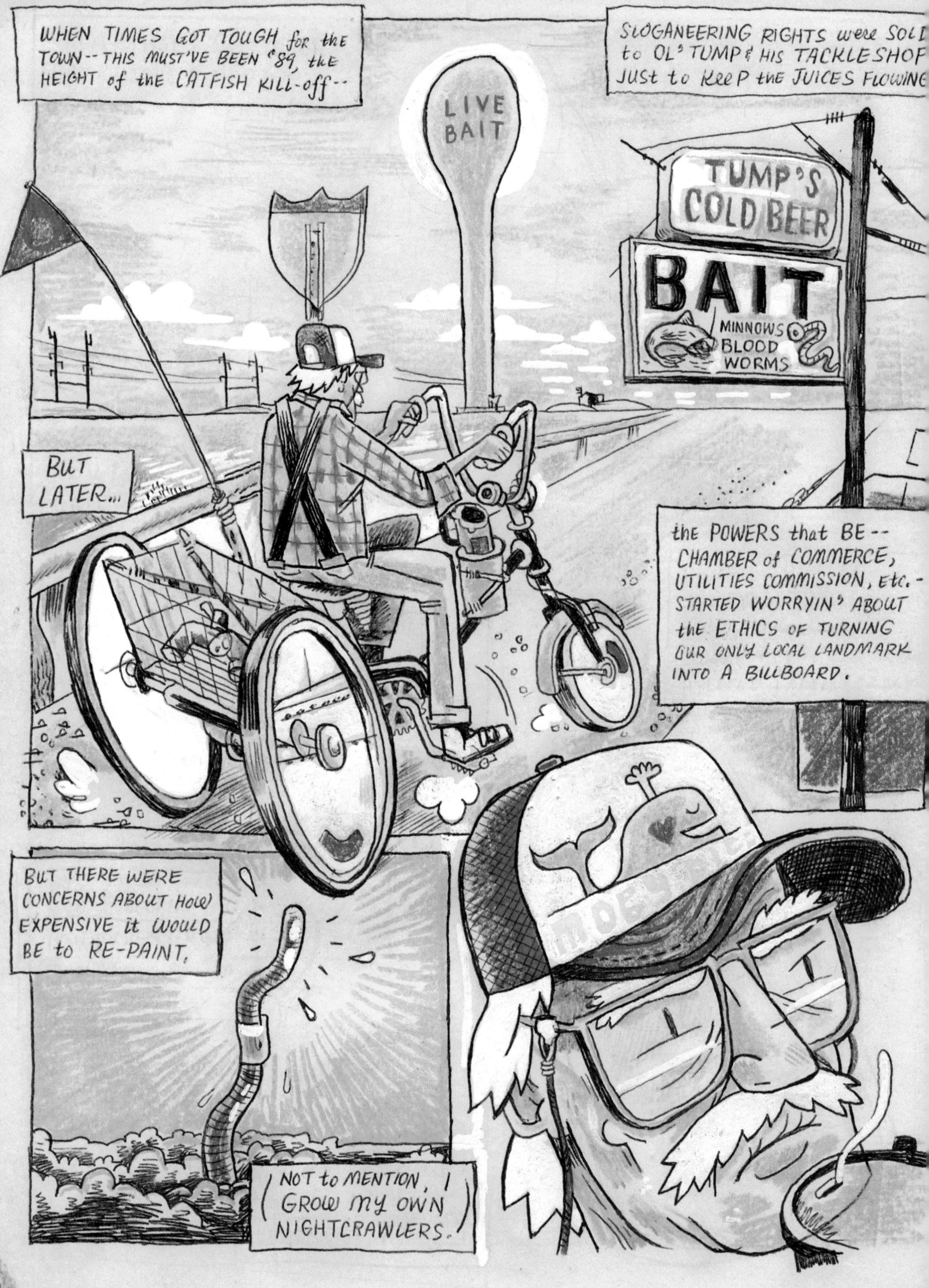
WHEN TIMES GOT TOUGH for the TOWN-- THIS MUST'VE BEEN '89, the HEIGHT of the CATFISH Kill-off--
SLOGANEERING RIGHTS were SOLD to OL' TUMP & HIS TACKLESHOP JUST to Keep the JUICES FLOWING
LIVE BAIT
TUMP'S COLD BEER
BAIT
MINNOWS
BLOOD WORMS
BUT LATER...
the POWERS that BE-- CHAMBER of COMMERCE, UTILITIES COMMISSION, etc.- STARTED WORRYIN' ABOUT the ETHICS OF TURNING OUR ONLY LOCAL LANDMARK INTO A BILLBOARD.
BUT THERE WERE CONCERNS ABOUT HOW EXPENSIVE it WOULD BE to RE-PAINT.
(NOT to MENTION, I GROW MY OWN NIGHTCRAWLERS.)

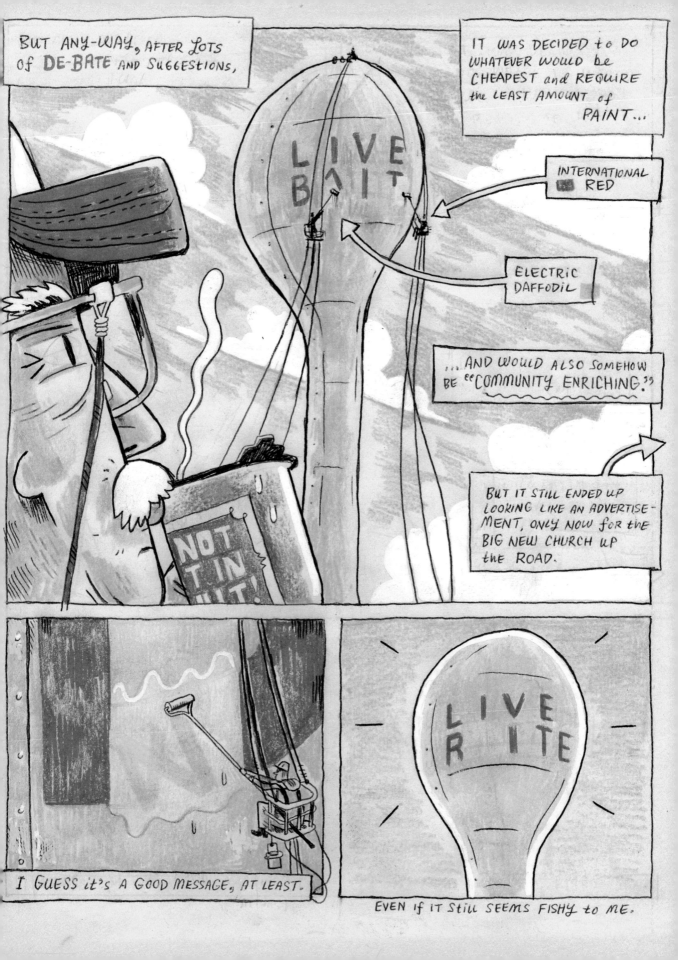

BUT ANY-WAY, AFTER LOTS OF **DE-BATE** AND SUGGESTIONS,

IT WAS DECIDED to DO WHATEVER WOULD be CHEAPEST and REQUIRE the LEAST AMOUNT of PAINT...

LIVE BAIT

INTERNATIONAL RED

ELECTRIC DAFFODIL

...AND WOULD ALSO SOMEHOW BE "COMMUNITY ENRICHING."

BUT IT STILL ENDED UP LOOKING LIKE AN ADVERTISE-MENT, ONLY NOW FOR THE BIG NEW CHURCH UP THE ROAD.

NOT IN MY...!

I GUESS it's A GOOD MESSAGE, AT LEAST.

LIVE RITE

EVEN IF IT STILL SEEMS FISHY to ME.

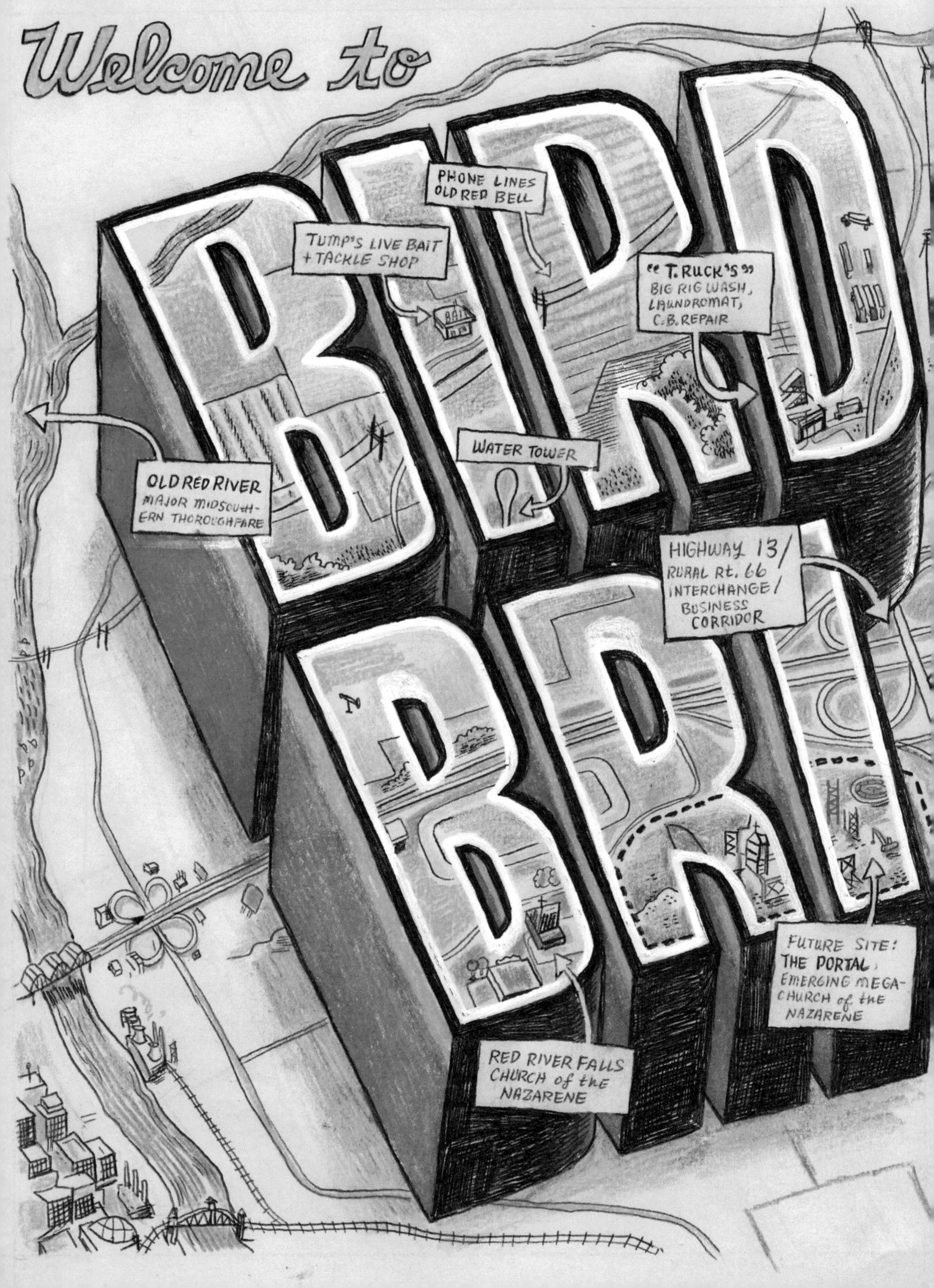
Welcome to
PHONE LINES
OLD RED BELL
TUMP'S LIVE BAIT + TACKLE SHOP
"T. RUCK'S" BIG RIG WASH, LAUNDROMAT, C.B. REPAIR
WATER TOWER
OLD RED RIVER
MAJOR MIDSOUTH-ERN THOROUGHFARE
HIGHWAY 13/ RURAL Rt. 66 INTERCHANGE/ BUSINESS CORRIDOR
FUTURE SITE: THE PORTAL, EMERGING MEGA-CHURCH of the NAZARENE
RED RIVER FALLS CHURCH of the NAZARENE

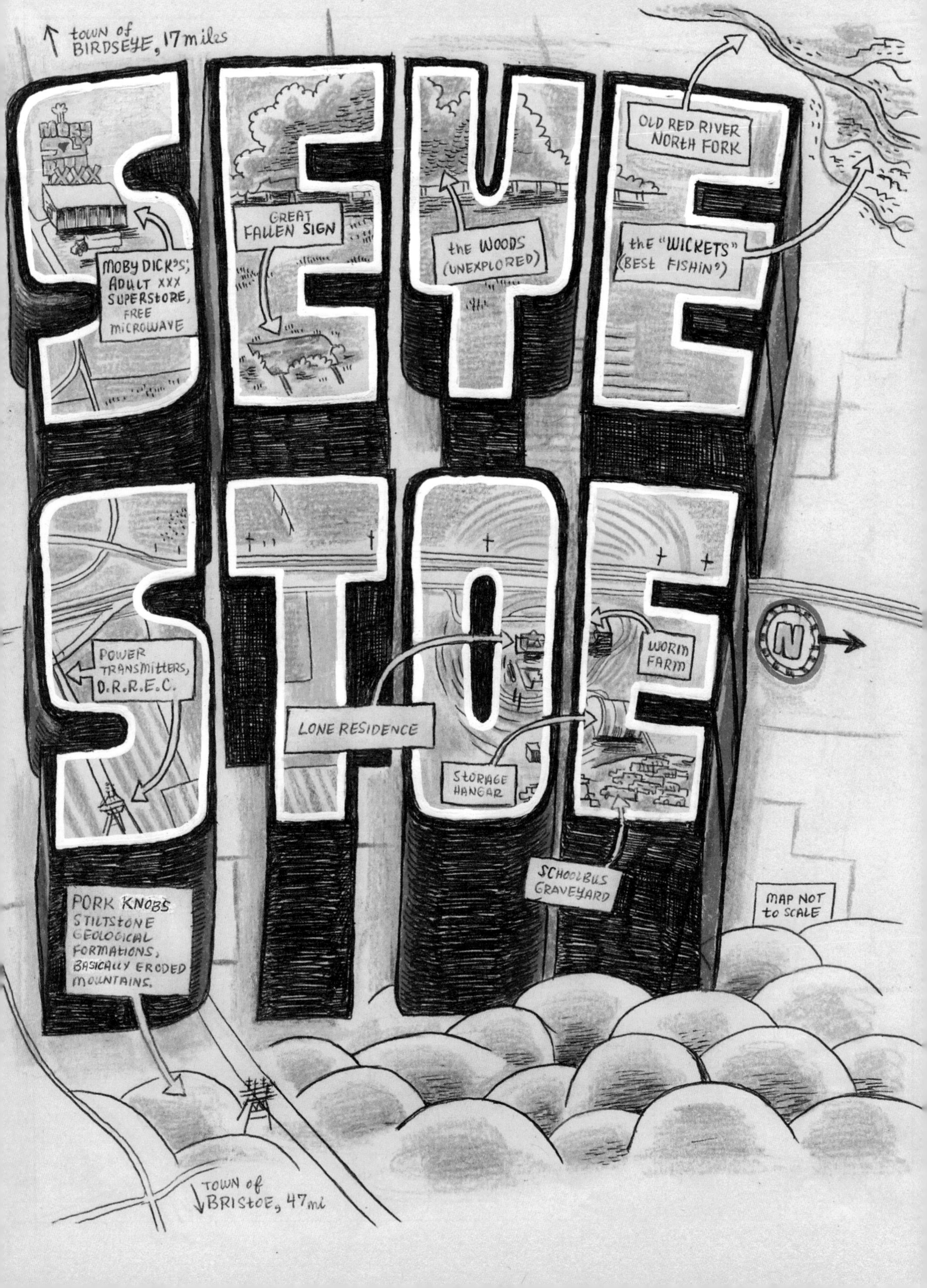
town of BIRDSEYE, 17 miles
SEYE STOE
MOBY DICK'S; ADULT XXX SUPERSTORE, FREE MICROWAVE
GREAT FALLEN SIGN
the WOODS (UNEXPLORED)
OLD RED RIVER NORTH FORK
the "WICKETS" (BEST FISHIN')
POWER TRANSMITTERS, D.R.R.E.C.
LONE RESIDENCE
WORM FARM
N
STORAGE HANGAR
SCHOOLBUS GRAVEYARD
MAP NOT to SCALE
PORK KNOBS STILTSTONE GEOLOGICAL FORMATIONS, BASICALLY ERODED MOUNTAINS.
TOWN of BRISTOE, 47 mi

Dramatis Personae.

BIRDSEYE BRISTOE *
A LANDOWNER

* NOT REAL NAME

KRYSTAL
HIS GREAT NIECE

Clint J Mungatroyd
HER COUSIN

NOT PICTURED: FARHAD, A BANDMATE

Family

BROTHER CLIFF M. JACKSON
A PASTOR, with Wife

STACE ▇▇▇▇ *
A CO-OWNER of an
ADULT SUPERSTORE

* IDENTITY PROTECTED

MR. SPECI

TUMP JR. ("TJ")
AN HEIR to A
LIVE BAIT FORTUNE

CHAMBER of COMMERCE

BIG TELECOM

the LADIES of EXCELLENCE
FEMALE ROLE MODELS
in INDUSTRY

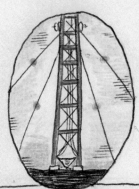

A STRANGER
WORLD'S TALLEST (GUYED) STRUCTURE
JULY 29 - AUGUST 28, 1998 *

* REASONS for COLLAPSE UNKNOWN

OUTSIDERS

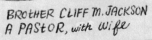

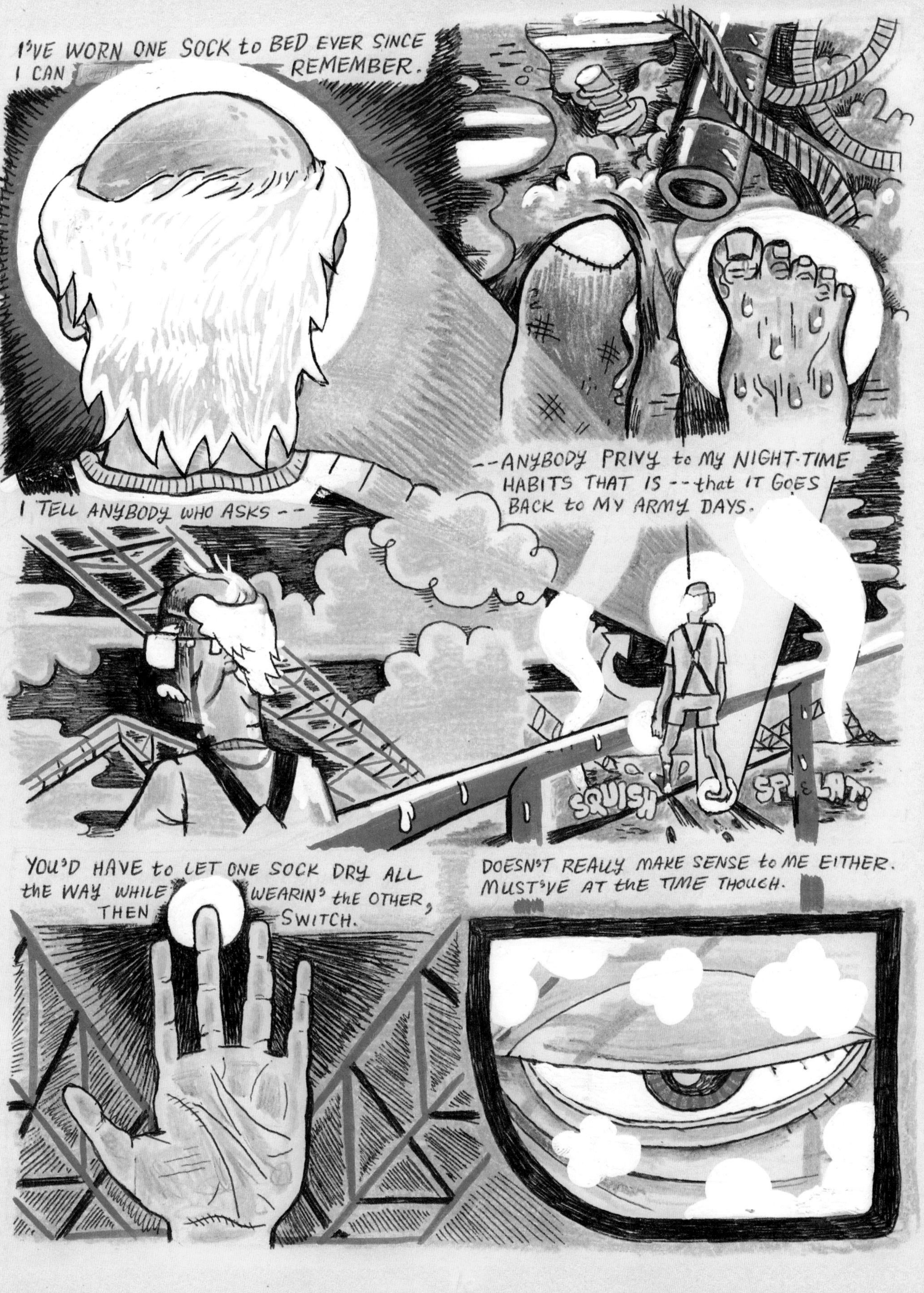
I'VE WORN ONE SOCK to BED EVER SINCE I CAN REMEMBER.
I TELL ANYBODY WHO ASKS --
--ANYBODY PRIVY to MY NIGHT-TIME HABITS THAT IS -- that IT GOES BACK to MY ARMY DAYS.
SQUISH
SPLAT
YOU'D HAVE to LET ONE SOCK DRY ALL the WAY WHILE WEARIN' the OTHER, THEN SWITCH.
DOESN'T REALLY MAKE SENSE to ME EITHER. MUST'VE AT the TIME THOUGH.

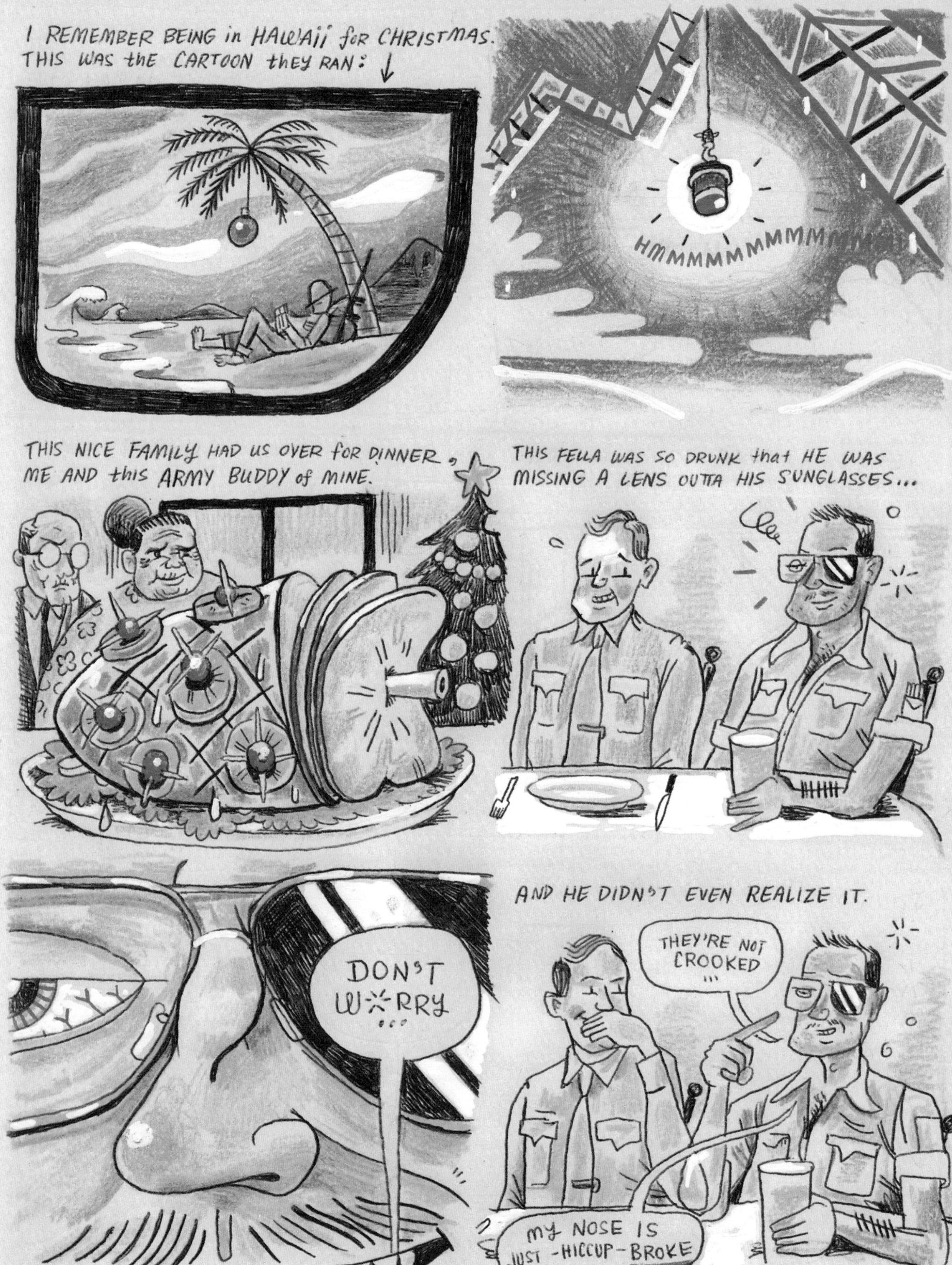
I REMEMBER BEING in HAWAii for CHRISTMAS. THIS WAS the CARTOON they RAN: ↓
HMMMMMMMMMMM
THIS NICE FAMILY HAD US OVER for DINNER, ME AND this ARMY BUDDY of MINE.
THIS FELLA WAS SO DRUNK that HE WAS MISSING A LENS OUTTA HIS SUNGLASSES...
DON'T WORRY...
AND HE DIDN'T EVEN REALIZE IT.
THEY'RE NOT CROOKED...
MY NOSE IS JUST -HICCUP- BROKE

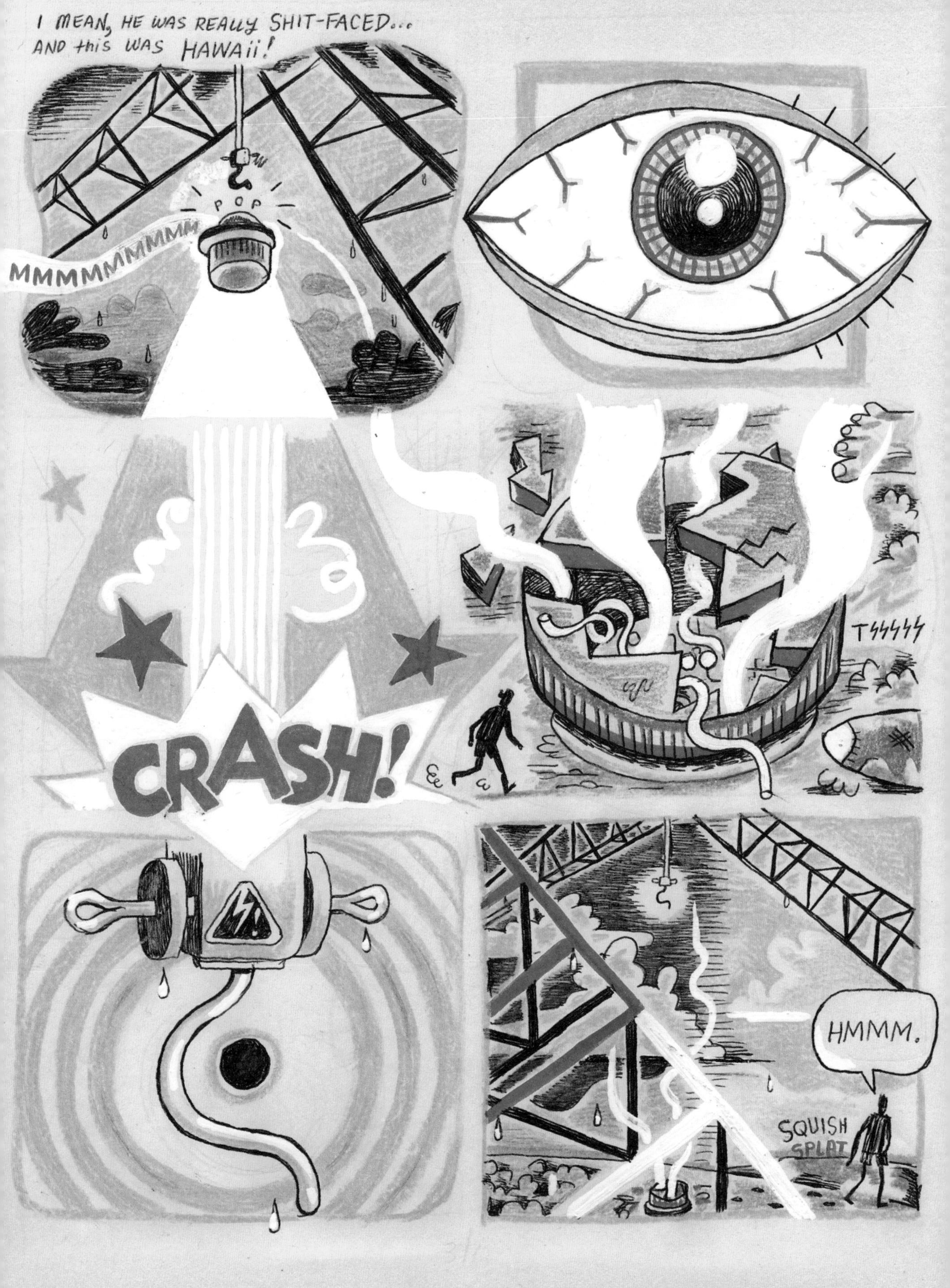
I MEAN, HE WAS REALLY SHIT-FACED...
AND this WAS HAWAii!
POP
MMMMMMMMMMM
CRASH!
TSSSSS
HMMM.
SQUISH
SPLAT

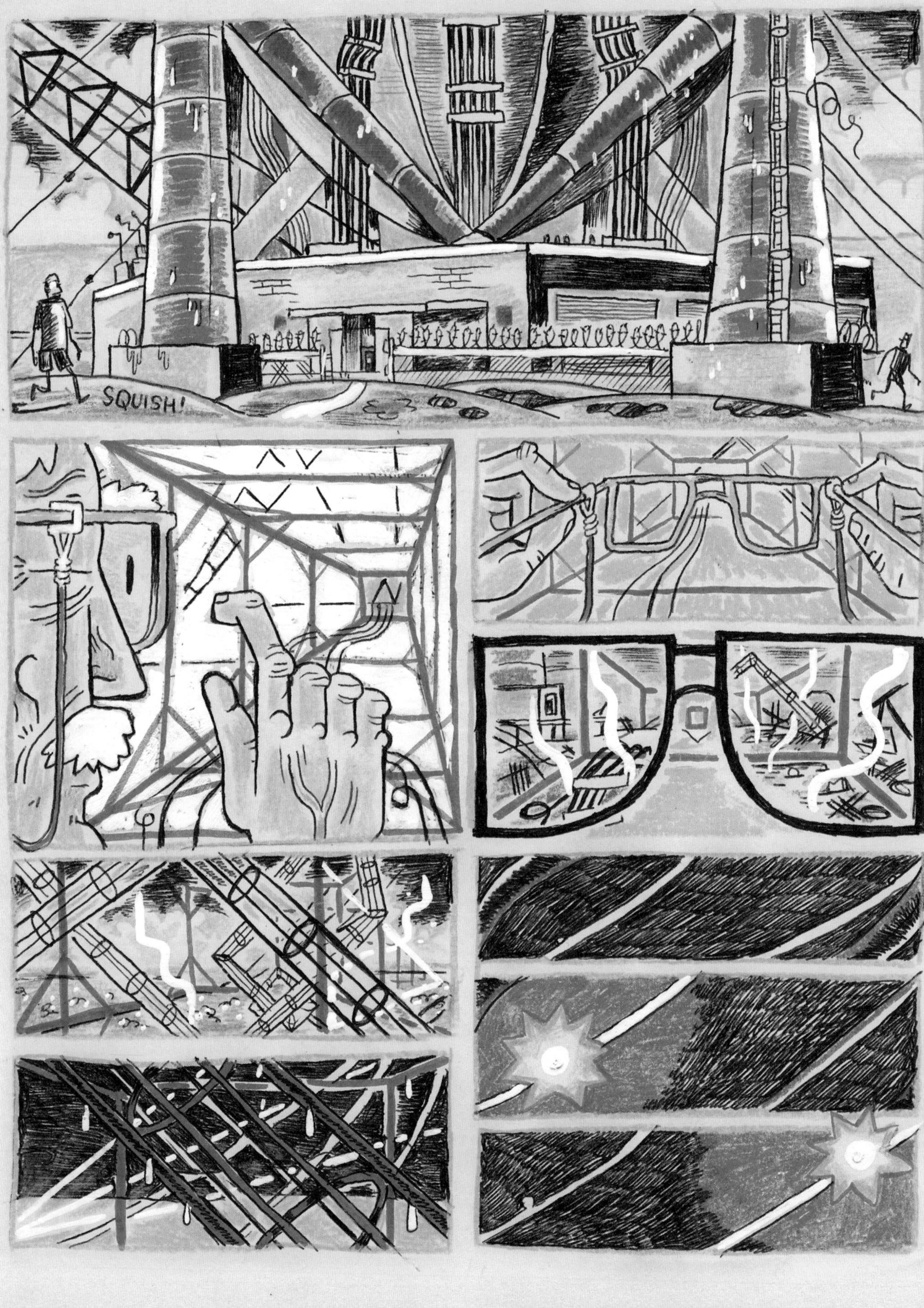
SQUISH!

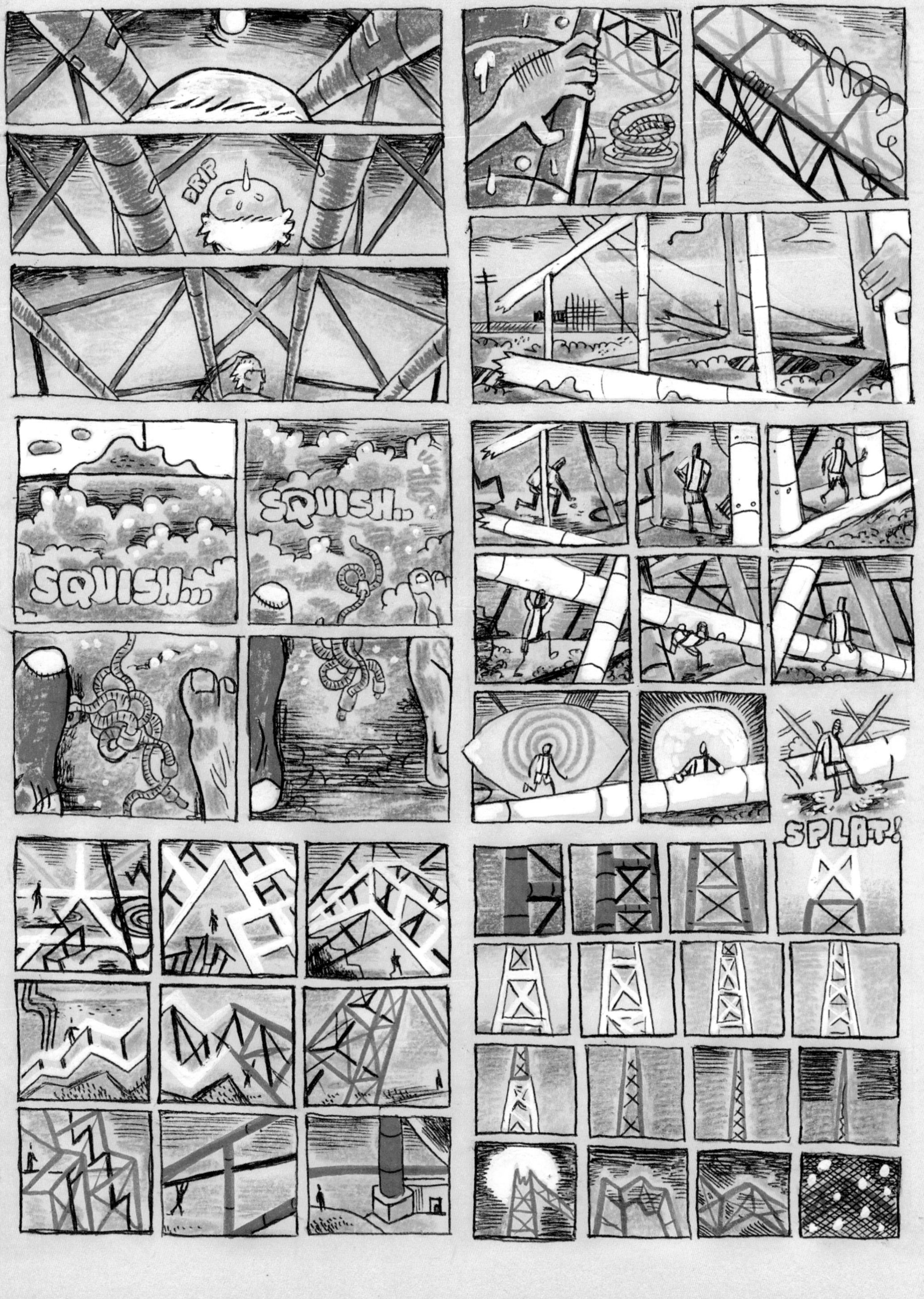
DRIP
SQUISH..
SQUISH..
SPLAT!

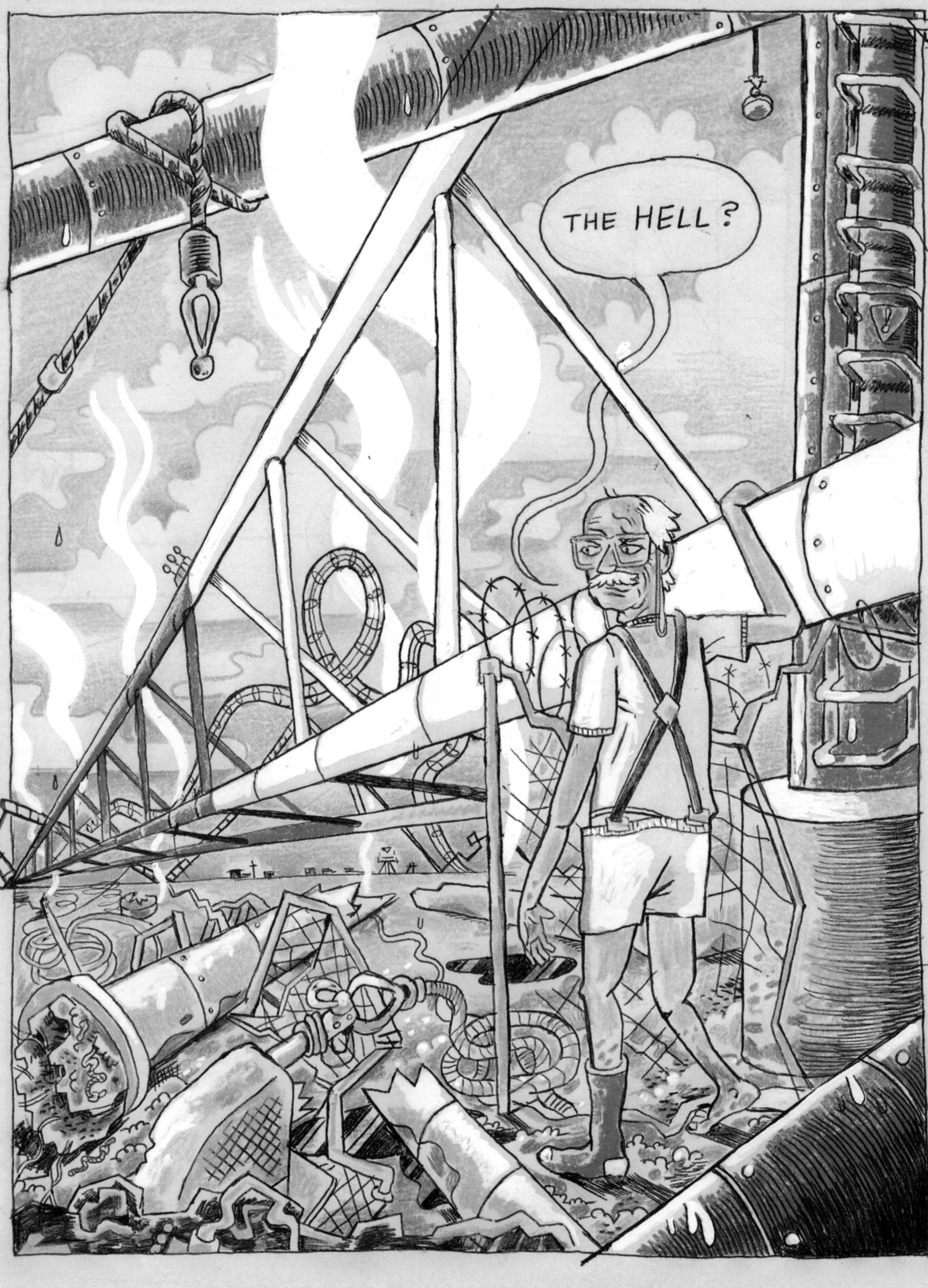
THE HELL ?

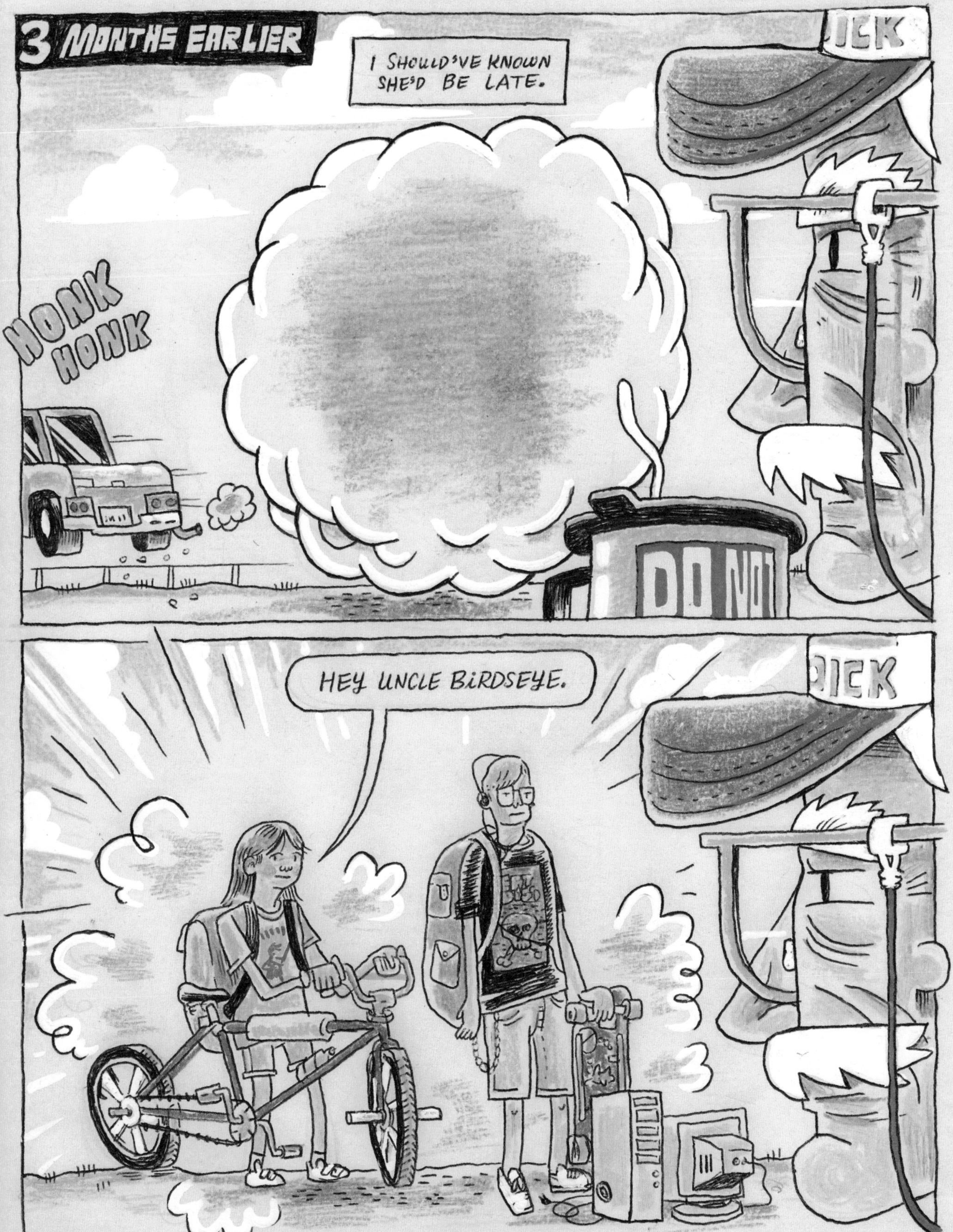
3 MONTHS EARLIER
I SHOULD'VE KNOWN SHE'D BE LATE.
HONK HONK
DO NOT
HEY UNCLE BIRDSEYE.

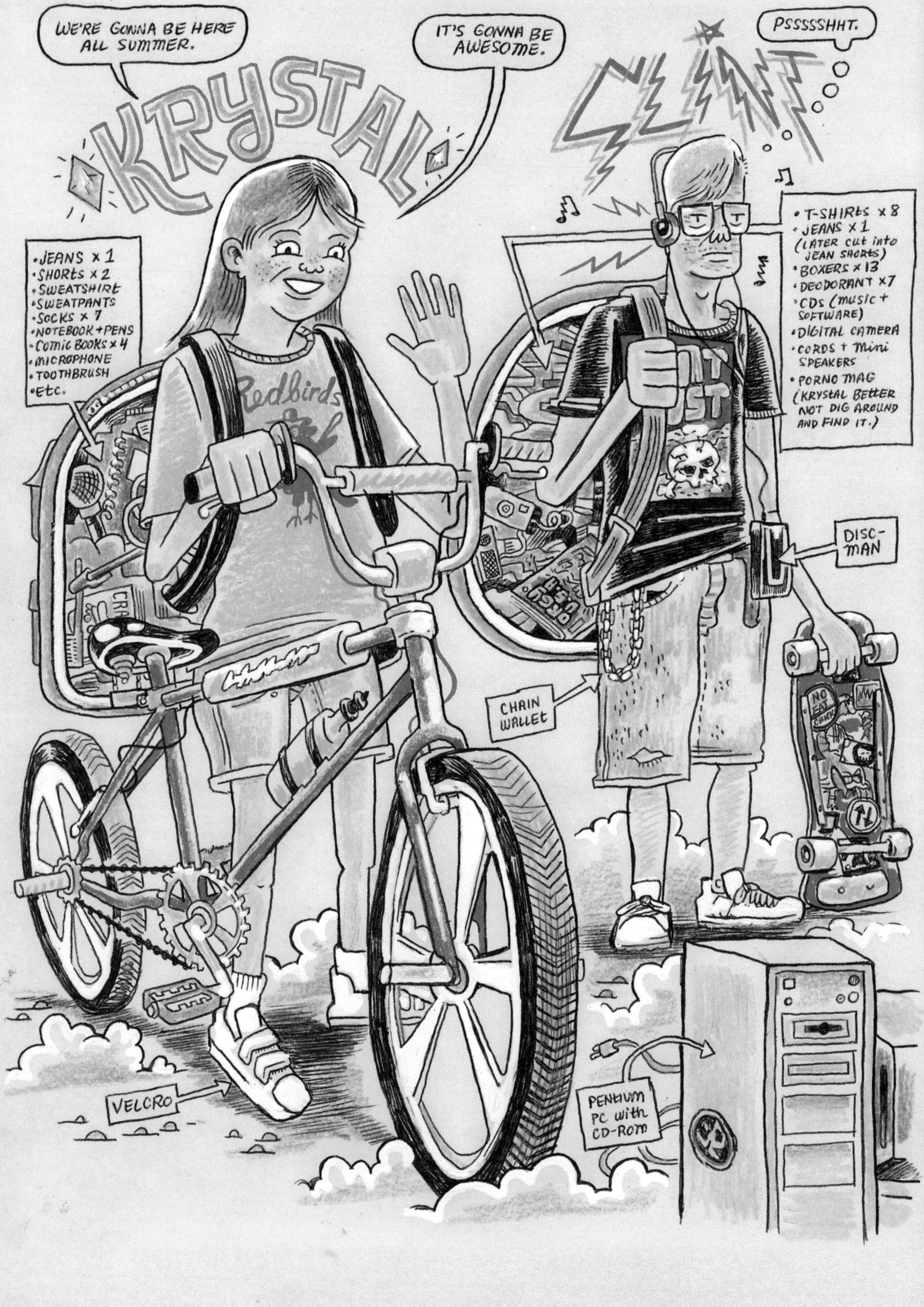
WE'RE GONNA BE HERE ALL SUMMER.
IT'S GONNA BE AWESOME.
PSSSSSHHT.
KRYSTAL
CLINT
•JEANS x 1
•SHORTS x 2
•SWEATSHIRT
•SWEATPANTS
•SOCKS x 7
•NOTEBOOK + PENS
•COMIC BOOKS x 4
•MICROPHONE
•TOOTHBRUSH
•ETC.
•T-SHIRTS x 8
•JEANS x 1 (LATER CUT INTO JEAN SHORTS)
•BOXERS x 13
•DEODORANT x 7
•CDS (MUSIC + SOFTWARE)
•DIGITAL CAMERA
•CORDS + MINI SPEAKERS
•PORNO MAG (KRYSTAL BETTER NOT DIG AROUND AND FIND IT.)
Redbirds
DISC-MAN
CHAIN WALLET
VELCRO
PENTIUM PC WITH CD-ROM

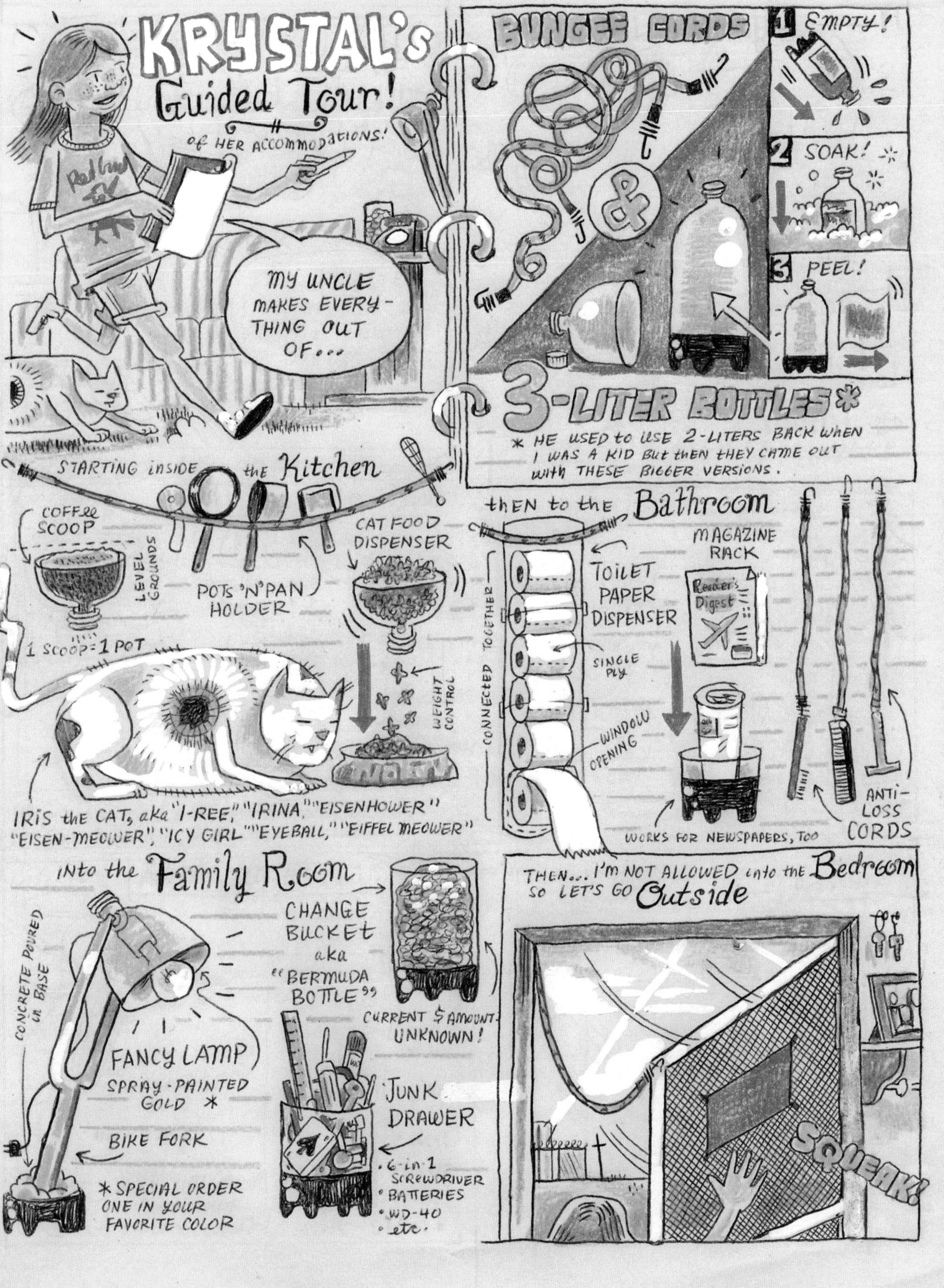

KRYSTAL'S Guided Tour!
of HER ACCOMMODATIONS!
MY UNCLE MAKES EVERY-THING OUT OF...
BUNGEE CORDS
&
1 EMPTY!
2 SOAK!
3 PEEL!
3-LITER BOTTLES*
* HE USED to USE 2-LITERS BACK WHEN I WAS A KID BUT THEN THEY CAME OUT WITH THESE BIGGER VERSIONS.
STARTING INSIDE THE Kitchen
COFFEE SCOOP
LEVEL GROUNDS
1 SCOOP=1 POT
POTS 'N' PAN HOLDER
CAT FOOD DISPENSER
WEIGHT CONTROL
IRIS THE CAT, aka "I-REE," "IRINA," "EISENHOWER" "EISEN-MEOWER," "ICY GIRL" "EYEBALL," "EIFFEL MEOWER"
then to the Bathroom
CONNECTED TOGETHER
TOILET PAPER DISPENSER
SINGLE PLY
WINDOW OPENING
MAGAZINE RACK
Reader's Digest
WORKS FOR NEWSPAPERS, TOO
ANTI-LOSS CORDS
INTO THE Family Room
CONCRETE POURED IN BASE
FANCY LAMP
SPRAY-PAINTED GOLD *
BIKE FORK
* SPECIAL ORDER ONE IN YOUR FAVORITE COLOR
CHANGE BUCKET aka "BERMUDA BOTTLE"
CURRENT $ AMOUNT UNKNOWN!
JUNK DRAWER
• 6-in-1 SCREWDRIVER
• BATTERIES
• WD-40
• etc.
THEN... I'M NOT ALLOWED into the Bedroom SO LET'S GO Outside
SQUEAK!

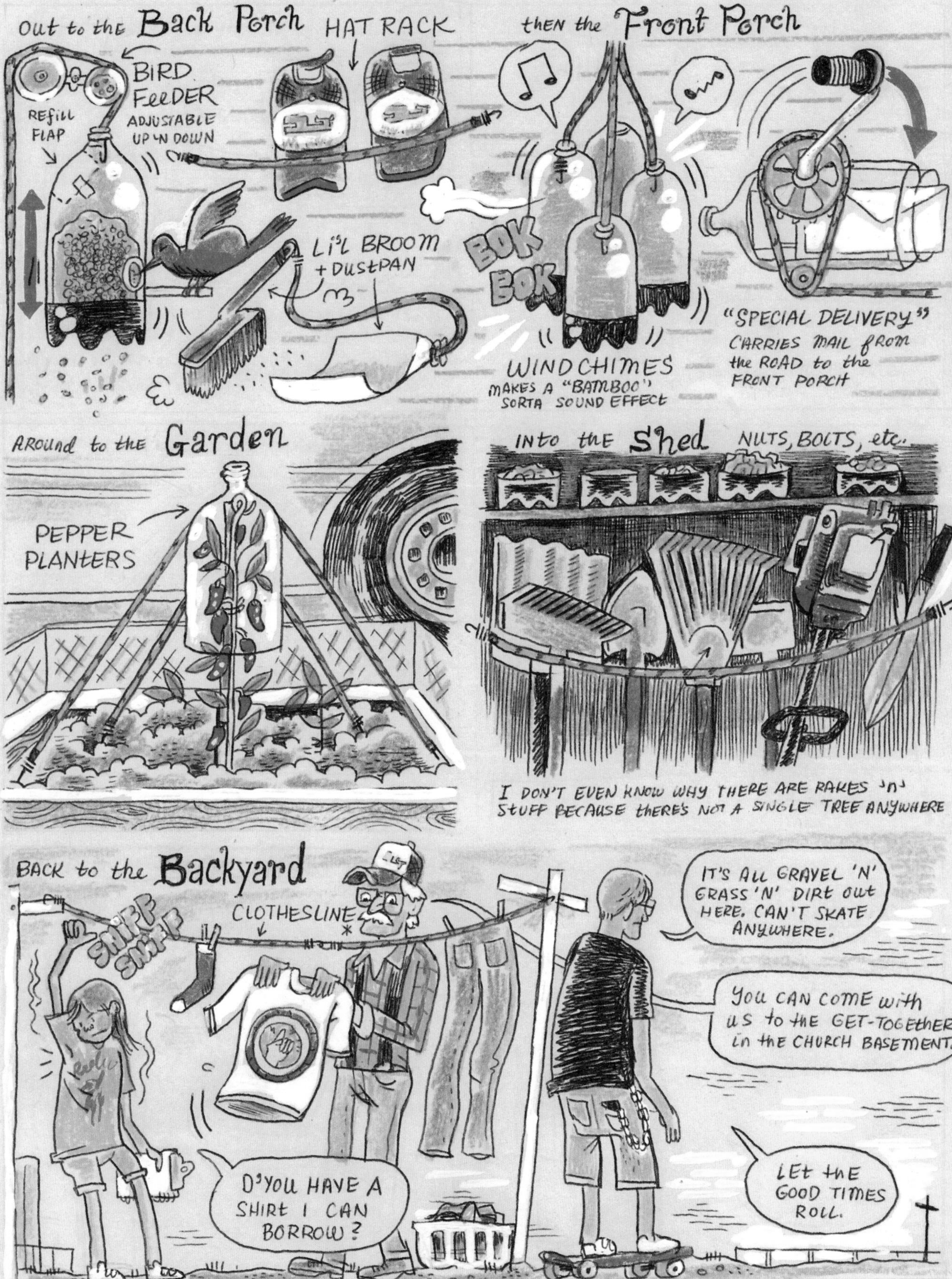

out to the Back Porch
HAT RACK
BIRD FEEDER
ADJUSTABLE UP 'N DOWN
REFILL FLAP
LI'L BROOM + DUSTPAN
then the Front Porch
BOK
BOK
WINDCHIMES
MAKES A "BAMBOO" SORTA SOUND EFFECT
"SPECIAL DELIVERY"
CARRIES MAIL FROM THE ROAD TO THE FRONT PORCH
AROUND to the Garden
PEPPER PLANTERS
into the Shed
NUTS, BOLTS, etc.
I DON'T EVEN KNOW WHY THERE ARE RAKES 'N' STUFF BECAUSE THERE'S NOT A SINGLE TREE ANYWHERE
BACK to the Backyard
CLOTHESLINE *
SNIFF SNIFF
IT'S ALL GRAVEL 'N' GRASS 'N' DIRT OUT HERE. CAN'T SKATE ANYWHERE.
YOU CAN COME WITH US TO THE GET-TOGETHER IN THE CHURCH BASEMENT.
D'YOU HAVE A SHIRT I CAN BORROW?
LET THE GOOD TIMES ROLL.
* NOT JUST A WRASSLIN' MOVE

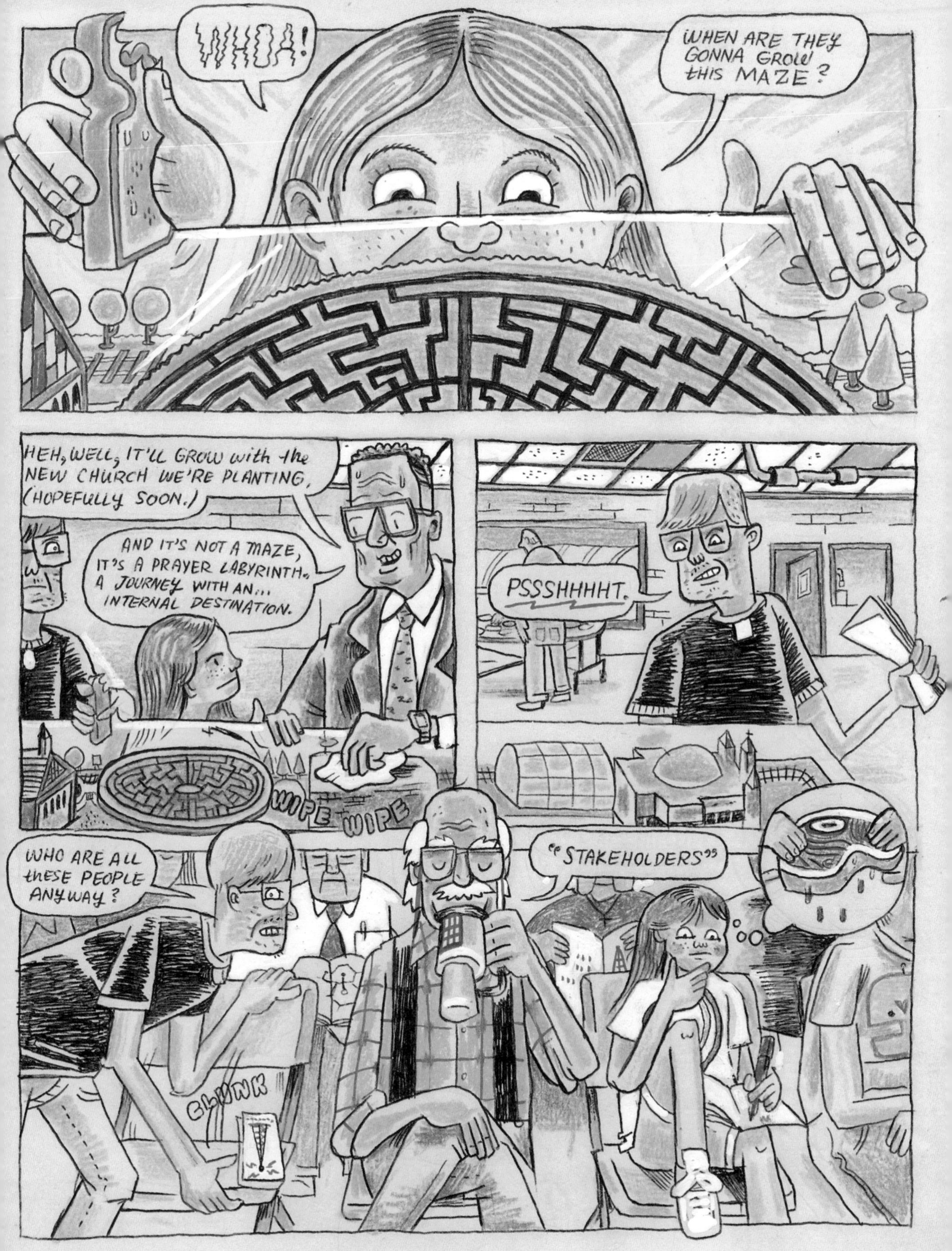
WHOA!
WHEN ARE THEY GONNA GROW THIS MAZE?
HEH, WELL, IT'LL GROW with the NEW CHURCH WE'RE PLANTING. (HOPEFULLY SOON.)
AND IT'S NOT A MAZE, IT'S A PRAYER LABYRINTH. A JOURNEY WITH AN... INTERNAL DESTINATION.
WIPE WIPE
PSSSHHHHT.
WHO ARE ALL these PEOPLE ANYWAY?
"STAKEHOLDERS"
CLUNK

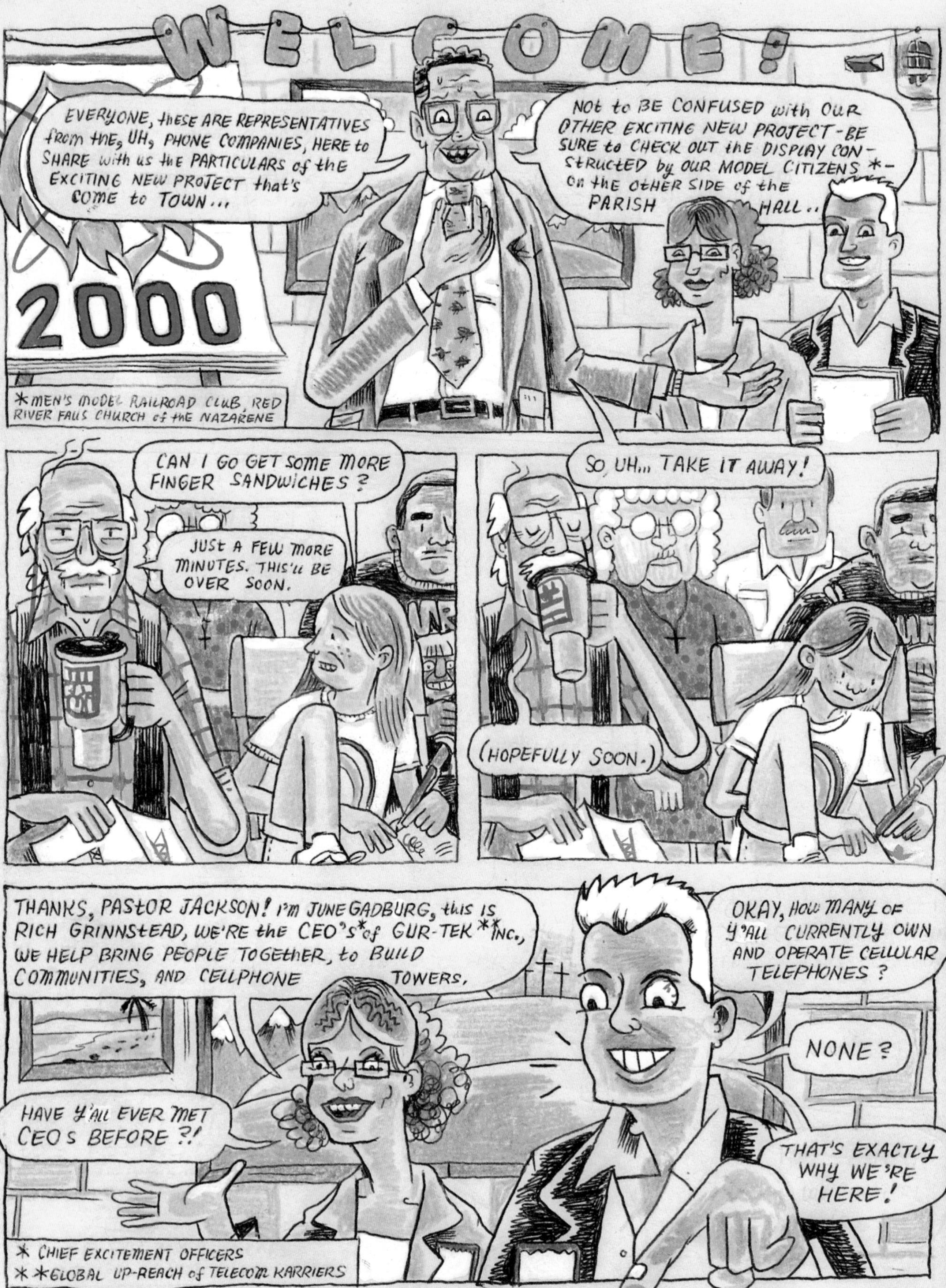
WELCOME!
2000
EVERYONE, THESE ARE REPRESENTATIVES FROM THE, UH, PHONE COMPANIES, HERE TO SHARE WITH US THE PARTICULARS OF THE EXCITING NEW PROJECT THAT'S COME TO TOWN...
NOT TO BE CONFUSED WITH OUR OTHER EXCITING NEW PROJECT - BE SURE TO CHECK OUT THE DISPLAY CONSTRUCTED BY OUR MODEL CITIZENS * - ON THE OTHER SIDE OF THE PARISH HALL..
* MEN'S MODEL RAILROAD CLUB, RED RIVER FALLS CHURCH OF THE NAZARENE
CAN I GO GET SOME MORE FINGER SANDWICHES?
JUST A FEW MORE MINUTES. THIS'LL BE OVER SOON.
SO, UH... TAKE IT AWAY!
(HOPEFULLY SOON.)
THANKS, PASTOR JACKSON! I'M JUNE GADBURG, THIS IS RICH GRINNSTEAD, WE'RE THE CEO'S* OF GUR-TEK** INC., WE HELP BRING PEOPLE TOGETHER, TO BUILD COMMUNITIES, AND CELLPHONE TOWERS.
OKAY, HOW MANY OF Y'ALL CURRENTLY OWN AND OPERATE CELLULAR TELEPHONES?
NONE?
HAVE Y'ALL EVER MET CEOS BEFORE?!
THAT'S EXACTLY WHY WE'RE HERE!
* CHIEF EXCITEMENT OFFICERS
** GLOBAL UP-REACH OF TELECOM KARRIERS

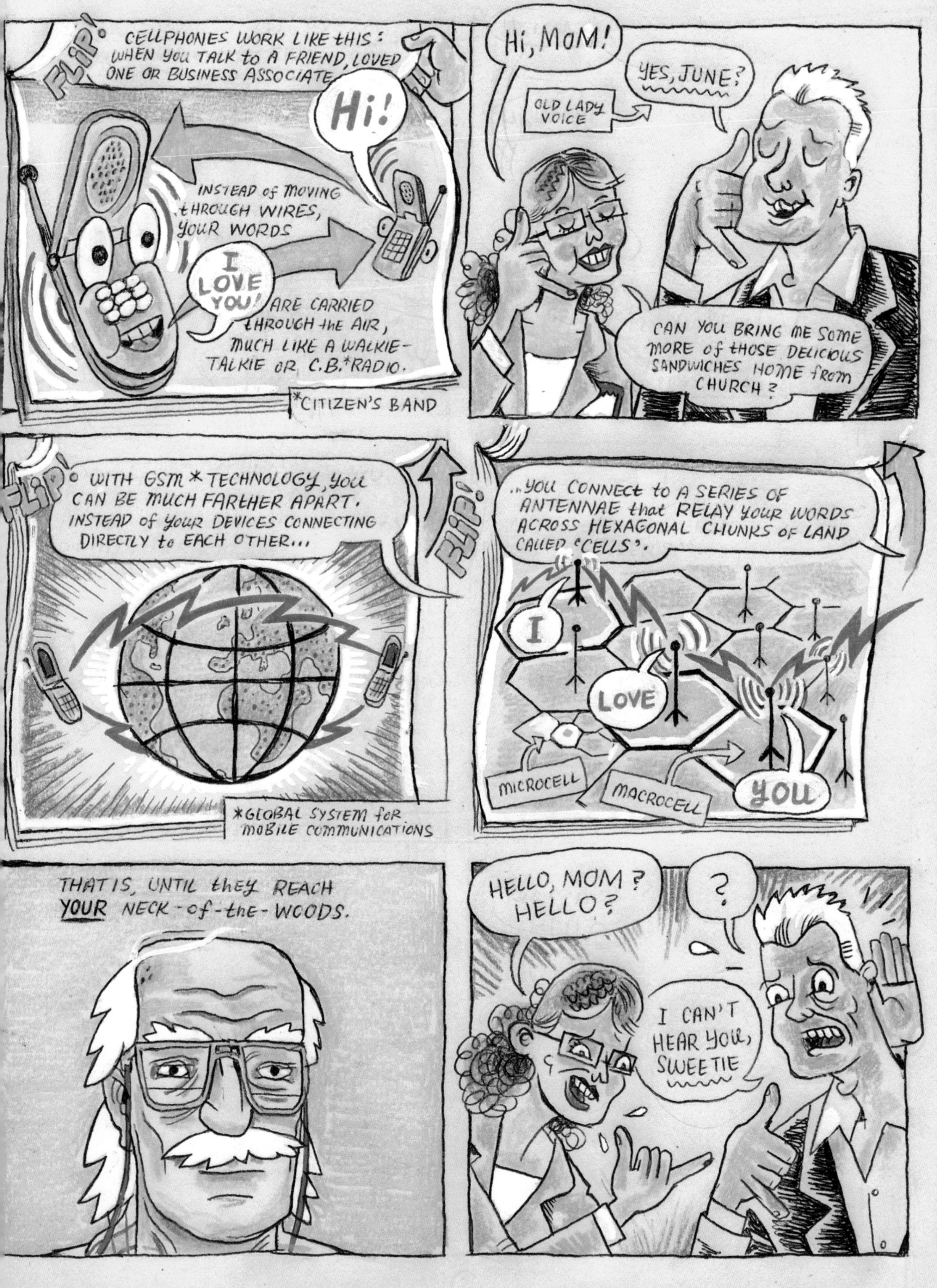
FLIP!
CELLPHONES WORK LIKE THIS: WHEN YOU TALK TO A FRIEND, LOVED ONE OR BUSINESS ASSOCIATE...
Hi!
INSTEAD OF MOVING THROUGH WIRES, YOUR WORDS
I LOVE YOU!
ARE CARRIED THROUGH THE AIR, MUCH LIKE A WALKIE-TALKIE OR C.B.* RADIO.
*CITIZEN'S BAND
Hi, MOM!
OLD LADY VOICE
YES, JUNE?
CAN YOU BRING ME SOME MORE OF THOSE DELICIOUS SANDWICHES HOME FROM CHURCH?
FLIP!
WITH GSM* TECHNOLOGY, YOU CAN BE MUCH FARTHER APART. INSTEAD OF YOUR DEVICES CONNECTING DIRECTLY TO EACH OTHER...
*GLOBAL SYSTEM FOR MOBILE COMMUNICATIONS
FLIP!
...YOU CONNECT TO A SERIES OF ANTENNAE THAT RELAY YOUR WORDS ACROSS HEXAGONAL CHUNKS OF LAND CALLED 'CELLS'.
I
LOVE
YOU
MICROCELL
MACROCELL
THAT IS, UNTIL THEY REACH YOUR NECK-OF-THE-WOODS.
HELLO, MOM? HELLO?
?
I CAN'T HEAR YOU, SWEETIE

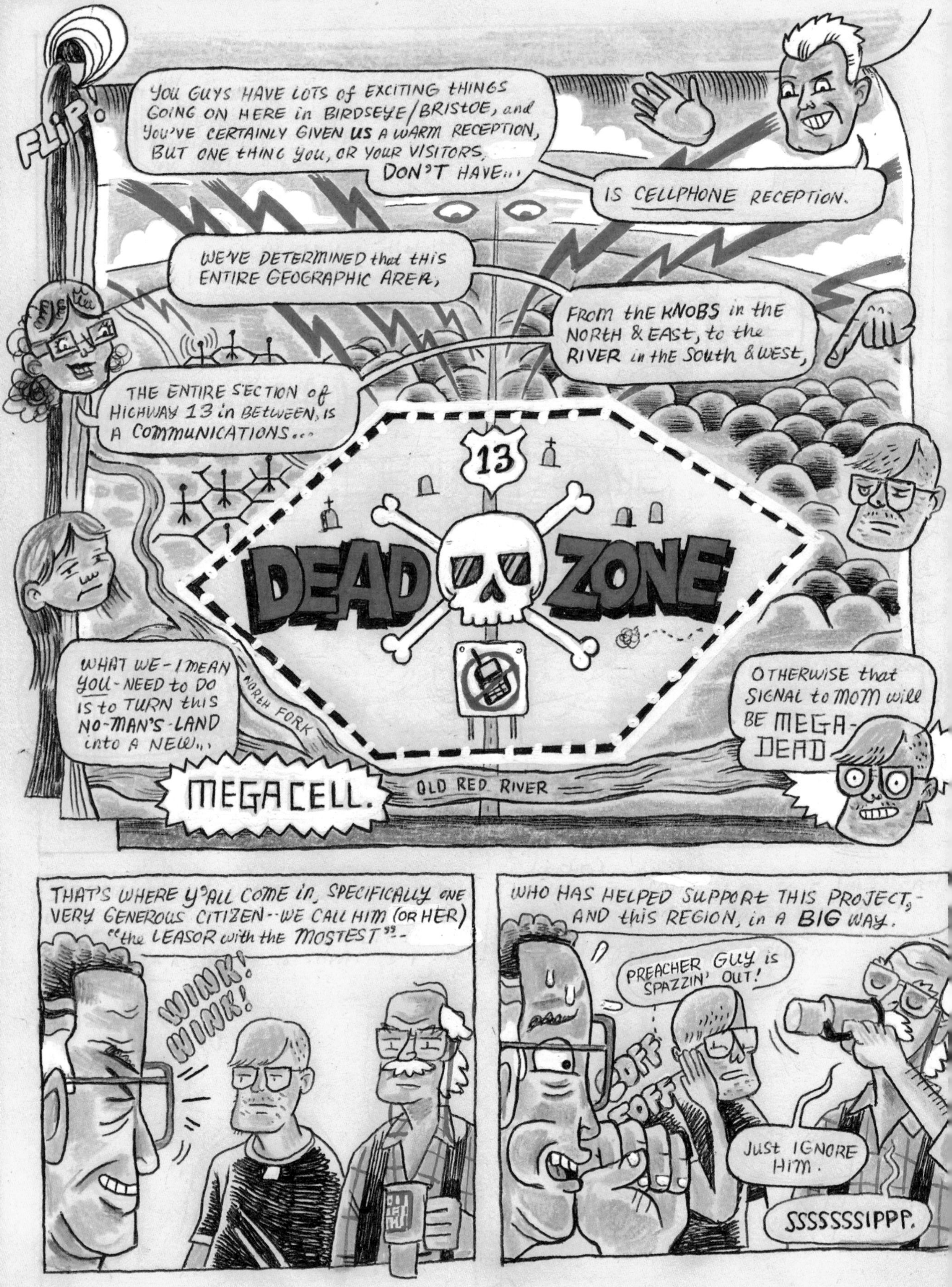
FLIP!
YOU GUYS HAVE LOTS OF EXCITING THINGS GOING ON HERE in BIRDSEYE/BRISTOE, and YOU'VE CERTAINLY GIVEN US A WARM RECEPTION, BUT ONE THING YOU, OR YOUR VISITORS, DON'T HAVE...
IS CELLPHONE RECEPTION.
WE'VE DETERMINED that this ENTIRE GEOGRAPHIC AREA,
FROM the KNOBS in the NORTH & EAST, to the RIVER in the South & WEST,
THE ENTIRE SECTION of HIGHWAY 13 in BETWEEN, IS A COMMUNICATIONS...
13
DEAD ZONE
WHAT WE - I MEAN YOU - NEED to DO is to TURN this NO-MAN'S-LAND into A NEW...
NORTH FORK
MEGACELL.
OLD RED RIVER
OTHERWISE that SIGNAL to MOM will BE MEGA-DEAD
THAT'S WHERE Y'ALL COME in, SPECIFICALLY ONE VERY GENEROUS CITIZEN--WE CALL HIM (OR HER) "the LEASOR with the MOSTEST"-
WINK! WINK!
WHO HAS HELPED SUPPORT THIS PROJECT,- AND this REGION, in A BIG WAY.
PREACHER GUY is SPAZZIN' OUT!
COFF COFF
Just IGNORE HIM.
SSSSSSSIPPP.

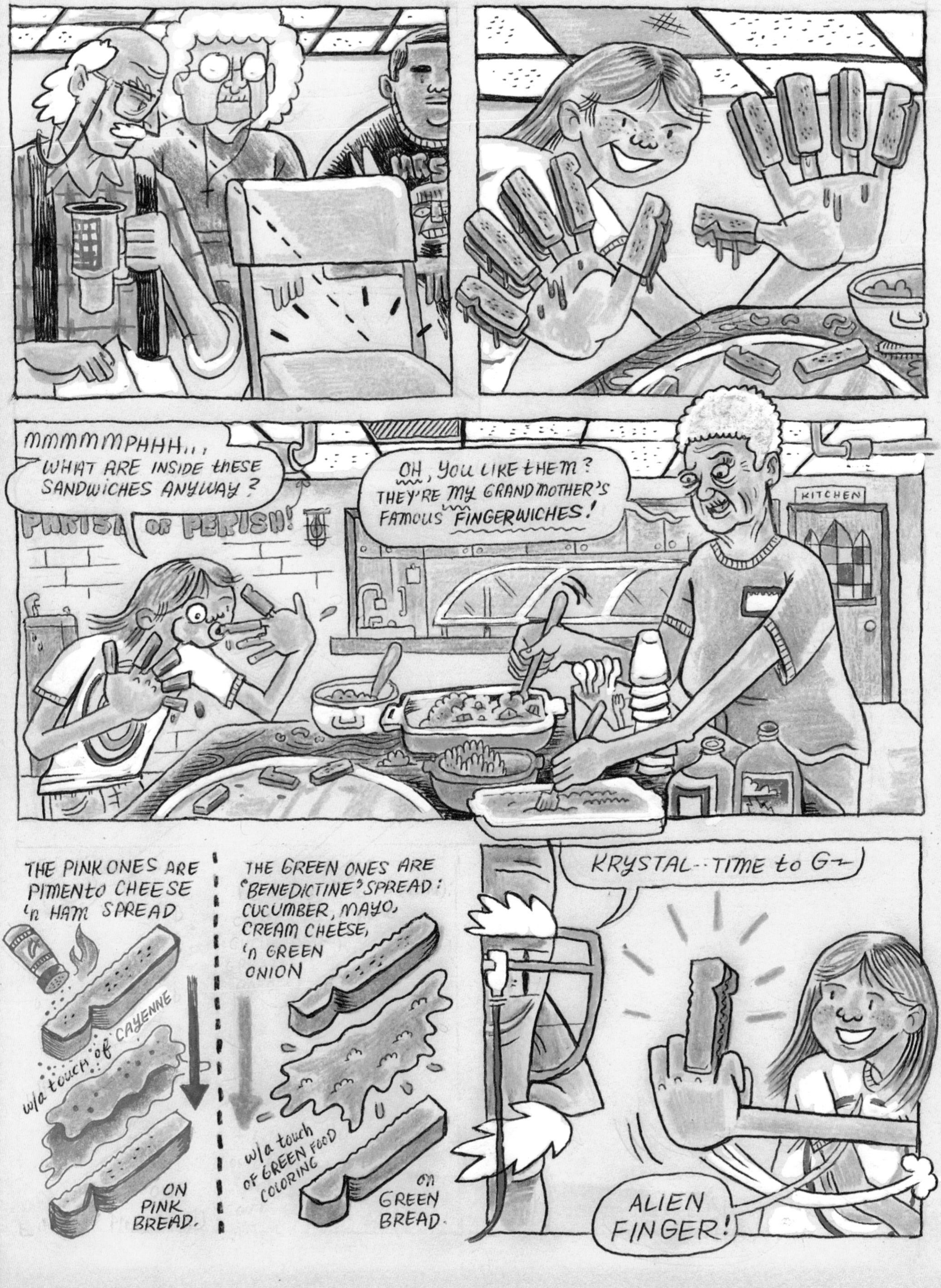
MMMMMMPHHH...
WHAT ARE INSIDE THESE SANDWICHES ANYWAY?
OH, YOU LIKE THEM? THEY'RE MY GRANDMOTHER'S FAMOUS FINGERWICHES!
KITCHEN
THE PINK ONES ARE PIMENTO CHEESE 'N HAM SPREAD
W/A TOUCH OF CAYENNE
ON PINK BREAD.
THE GREEN ONES ARE "BENEDICTINE" SPREAD: CUCUMBER, MAYO, CREAM CHEESE, 'N GREEN ONION
W/A TOUCH OF GREEN FOOD COLORING
ON GREEN BREAD.
KRYSTAL-- TIME TO G--
ALIEN FINGER!

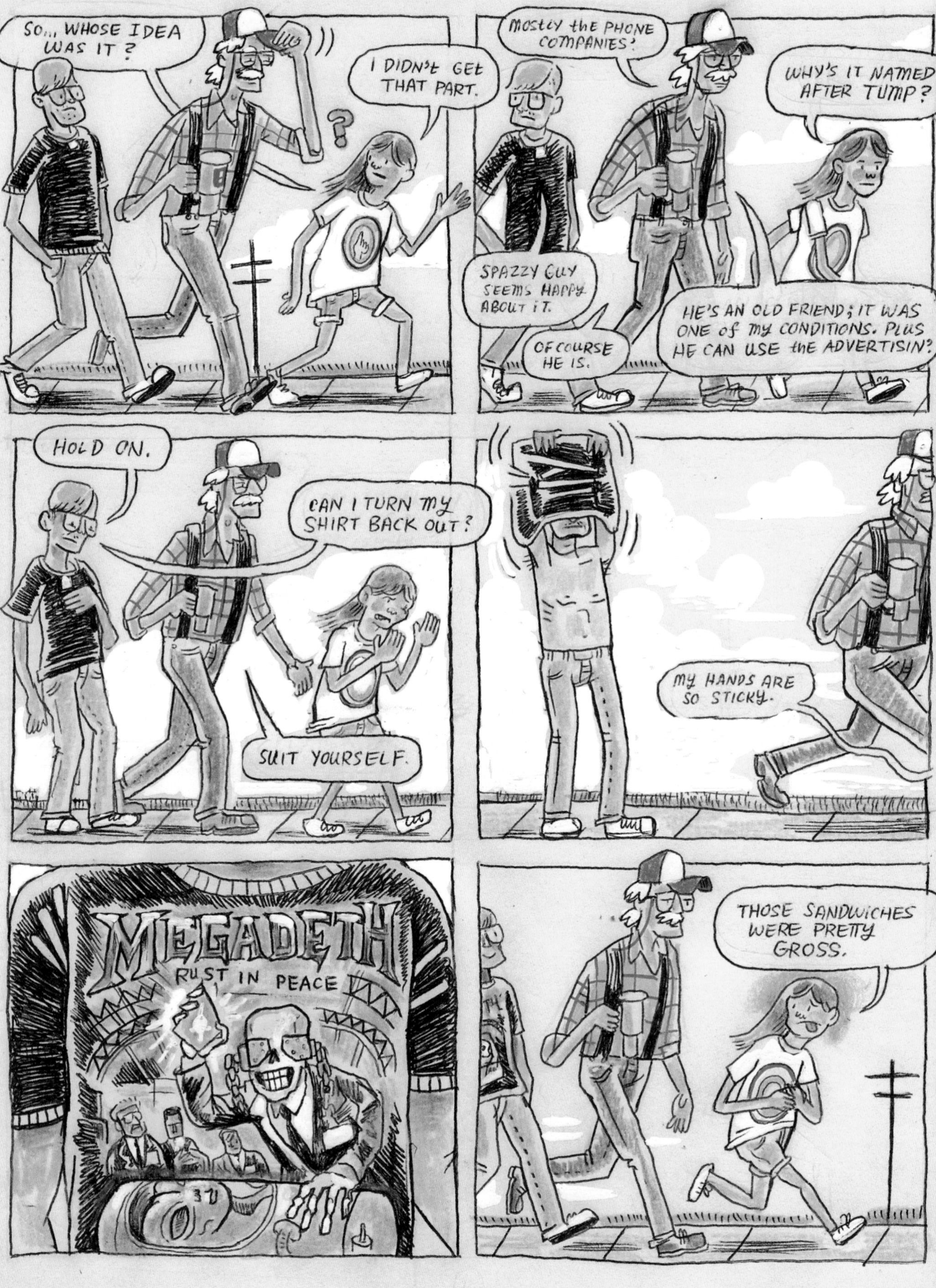
SO... WHOSE IDEA WAS IT?
I DIDN'T GET THAT PART.
?
MOSTLY THE PHONE COMPANIES.
WHY'S IT NAMED AFTER TUMP?
SPAZZY GUY SEEMS HAPPY ABOUT IT.
OF COURSE HE IS.
HE'S AN OLD FRIEND; IT WAS ONE OF MY CONDITIONS. PLUS HE CAN USE THE ADVERTISING.
HOLD ON.
CAN I TURN MY SHIRT BACK OUT?
SUIT YOURSELF.
MY HANDS ARE SO STICKY.
MEGADETH
RUST IN PEACE
THOSE SANDWICHES WERE PRETTY GROSS.

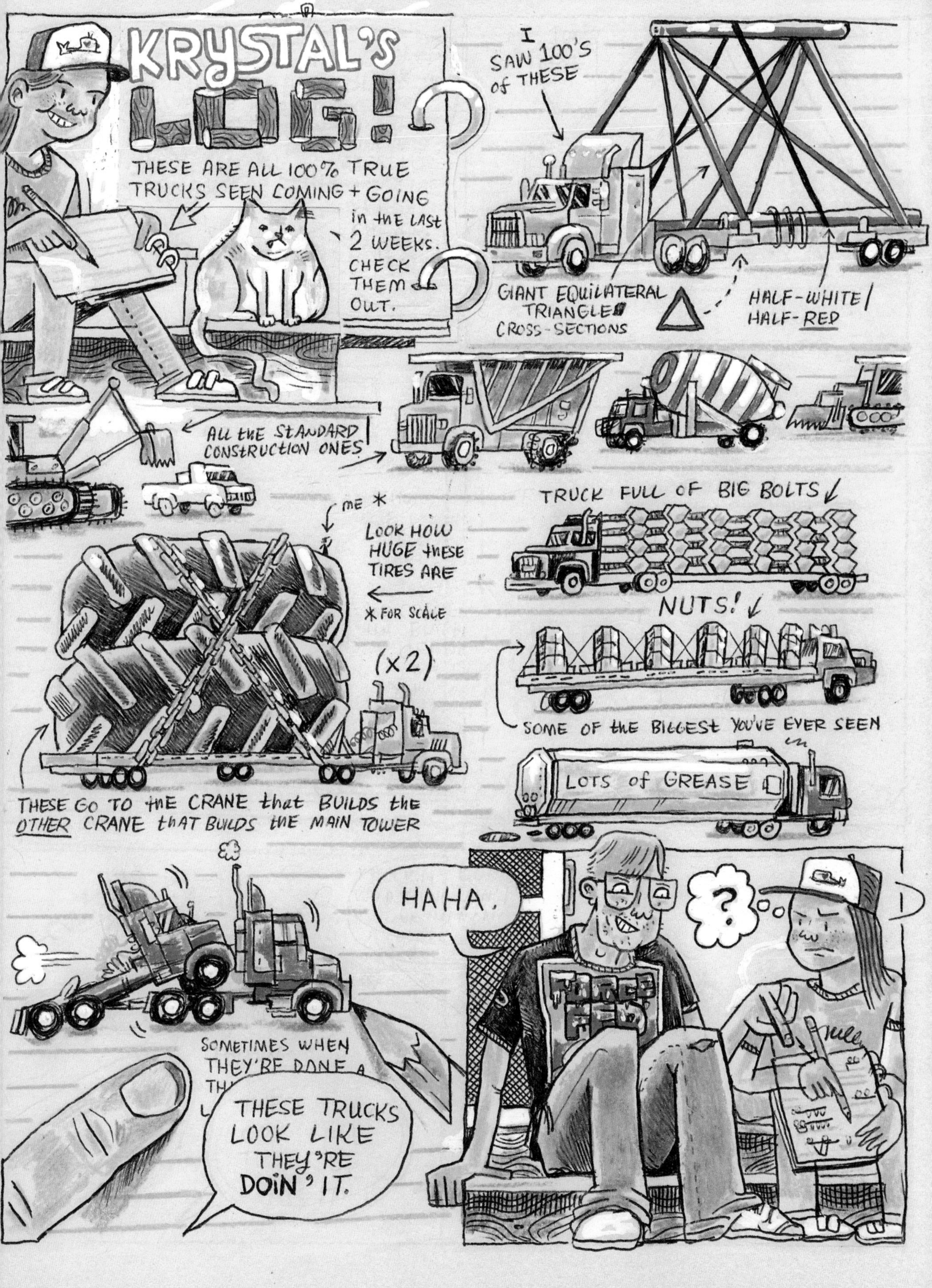

KRYSTAL'S LOG!
THESE ARE ALL 100% TRUE TRUCKS SEEN COMING + GOING in the LAST 2 WEEKS. CHECK THEM OUT.
I SAW 100'S of THESE
GIANT EQUILATERAL TRIANGLE CROSS-SECTIONS
HALF-WHITE / HALF-RED
ALL the STANDARD CONSTRUCTION ONES
TRUCK FULL OF BIG BOLTS
me *
LOOK HOW HUGE these TIRES ARE
* FOR SCALE
(x2)
THESE GO TO the CRANE that BUILDS the OTHER CRANE that BUILDS the MAIN TOWER
NUTS!
SOME OF the BIGGEST YOU'VE EVER SEEN
LOTS of GREASE
SOMETIMES WHEN
THEY'RE DONE A
THESE TRUCKS LOOK LIKE THEY'RE DOIN' IT.
HAHA.
?

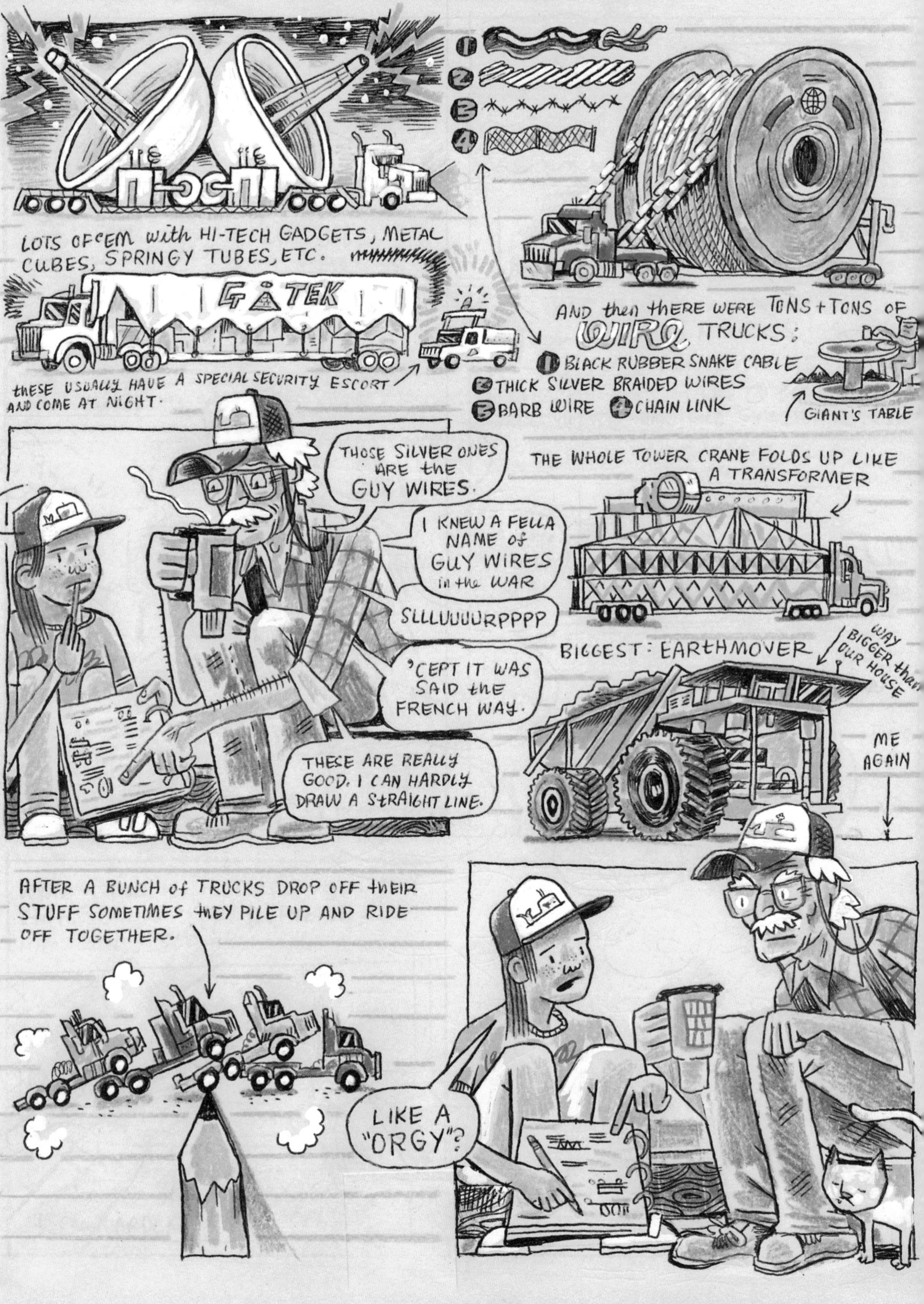

LOTS OF 'EM WITH HI-TECH GADGETS, METAL CUBES, SPRINGY TUBES, ETC.
GTEK
THESE USUALLY HAVE A SPECIAL SECURITY ESCORT AND COME AT NIGHT.
1
2
3
4
AND THEN THERE WERE TONS + TONS OF WIRE TRUCKS:
1 BLACK RUBBER SNAKE CABLE
2 THICK SILVER BRAIDED WIRES
3 BARB WIRE 4 CHAIN LINK
GIANT'S TABLE
THOSE SILVER ONES ARE THE GUY WIRES.
I KNEW A FELLA NAME OF GUY WIRES IN THE WAR
SLLLUUUURPPPP
'CEPT IT WAS SAID THE FRENCH WAY.
THESE ARE REALLY GOOD. I CAN HARDLY DRAW A STRAIGHT LINE.
THE WHOLE TOWER CRANE FOLDS UP LIKE A TRANSFORMER
BIGGEST: EARTHMOVER
WAY BIGGER THAN OUR HOUSE
ME AGAIN
AFTER A BUNCH OF TRUCKS DROP OFF THEIR STUFF SOMETIMES THEY PILE UP AND RIDE OFF TOGETHER.
LIKE A "ORGY"?

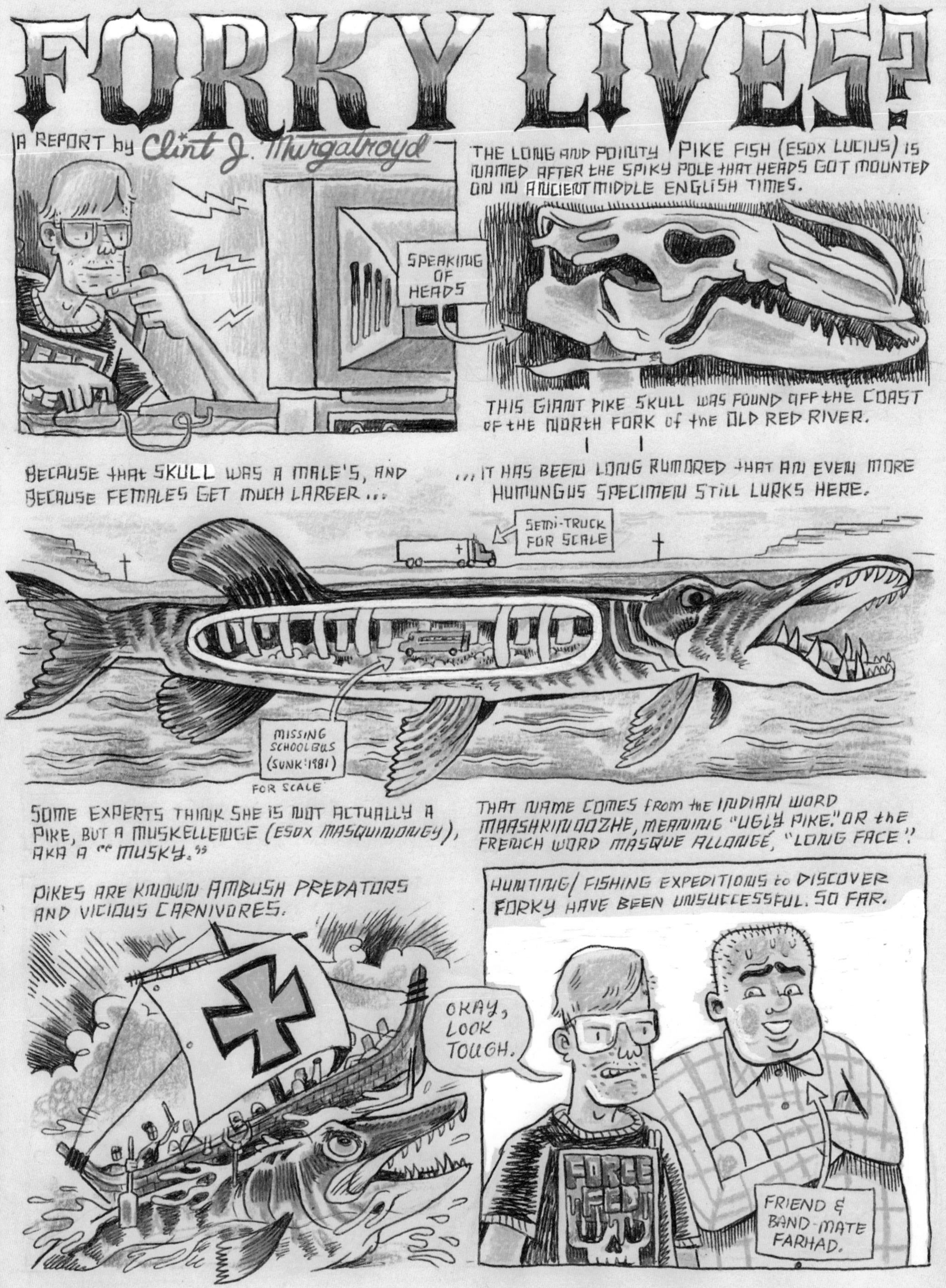
FORKY LIVES?
A REPORT by Clint J. Murgatroyd
THE LONG AND POINTY PIKE FISH (ESOX LUCIUS) IS NAMED AFTER THE SPIKY POLE THAT HEADS GOT MOUNTED ON IN ANCIENT MIDDLE ENGLISH TIMES.
SPEAKING OF HEADS
THIS GIANT PIKE SKULL WAS FOUND OFF THE COAST OF THE NORTH FORK OF THE OLD RED RIVER.
BECAUSE THAT SKULL WAS A MALE'S, AND BECAUSE FEMALES GET MUCH LARGER...
...IT HAS BEEN LONG RUMORED THAT AN EVEN MORE HUMUNGUS SPECIMEN STILL LURKS HERE.
SEMI-TRUCK FOR SCALE
MISSING SCHOOLBUS (SUNK: 1981)
FOR SCALE
SOME EXPERTS THINK SHE IS NOT ACTUALLY A PIKE, BUT A MUSKELLENGE (ESOX MASQUINONGY), AKA A "MUSKY."
THAT NAME COMES FROM THE INDIAN WORD MAASHKINOOZHE, MEANING "UGLY PIKE," OR THE FRENCH WORD MASQUE ALLONGÉ, "LONG FACE."
PIKES ARE KNOWN AMBUSH PREDATORS AND VICIOUS CARNIVORES.
HUNTING/FISHING EXPEDITIONS TO DISCOVER FORKY HAVE BEEN UNSUCCESSFUL. SO FAR.
OKAY, LOOK TOUGH.
FORCE FED
FRIEND & BAND-MATE FARHAD.

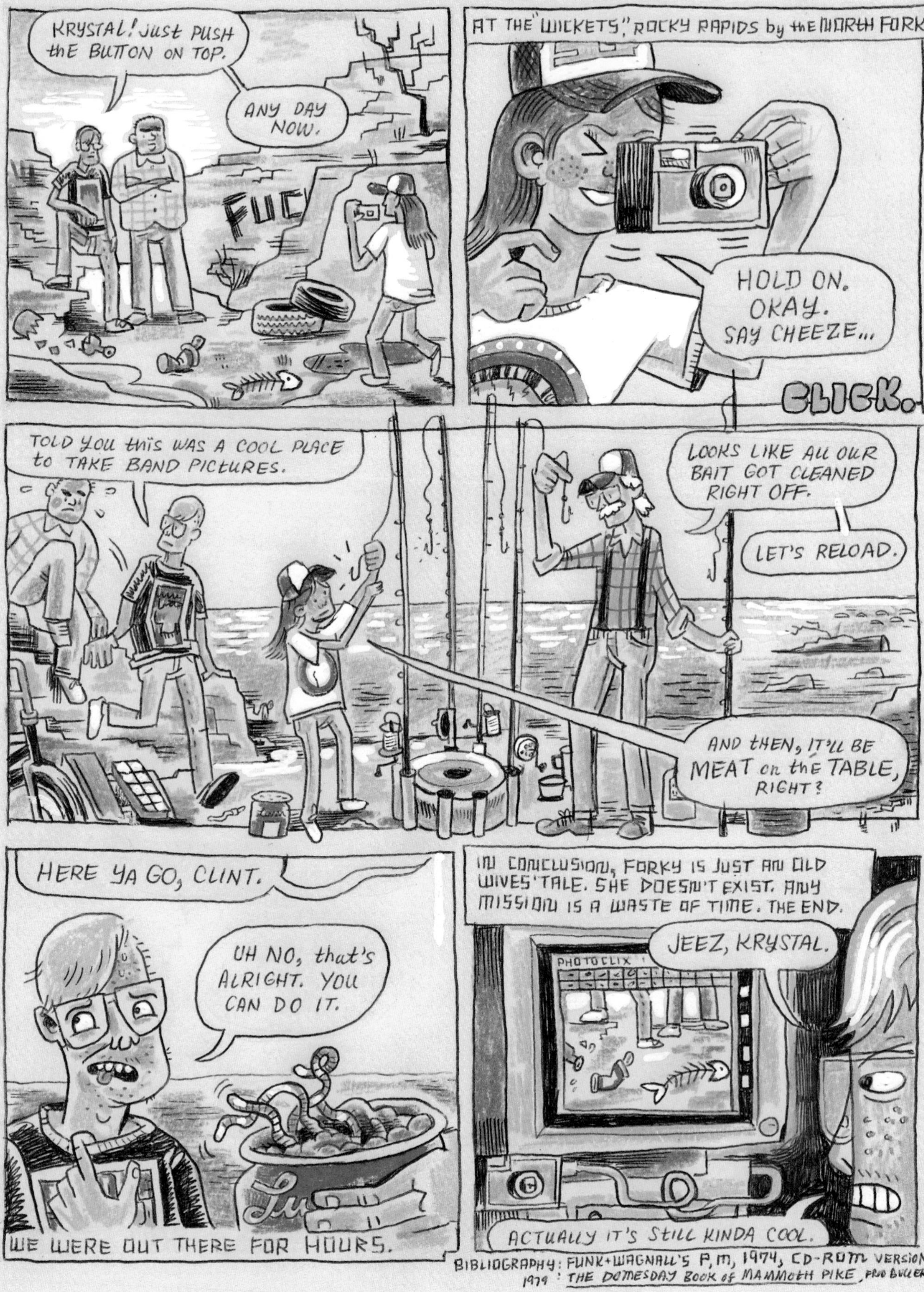
KRYSTAL! JUST PUSH THE BUTTON ON TOP.
ANY DAY NOW.
FUC
AT THE "WICKETS," ROCKY RAPIDS BY THE NORTH FORK.
HOLD ON. OKAY. SAY CHEEZE...
CLICK.
TOLD YOU THIS WAS A COOL PLACE TO TAKE BAND PICTURES.
LOOKS LIKE ALL OUR BAIT GOT CLEANED RIGHT OFF.
LET'S RELOAD.
AND THEN, IT'LL BE MEAT ON THE TABLE, RIGHT?
HERE YA GO, CLINT.
UH NO, THAT'S ALRIGHT. YOU CAN DO IT.
WE WERE OUT THERE FOR HOURS.
IN CONCLUSION, FORKY IS JUST AN OLD WIVES' TALE. SHE DOESN'T EXIST. ANY MISSION IS A WASTE OF TIME. THE END.
JEEZ, KRYSTAL.
PHOTOCLIX
ACTUALLY IT'S STILL KINDA COOL.

BIBLIOGRAPHY: FUNK+WAGNALL'S P,M, 1974, CD-ROM VERSION
1979 : THE DOMESDAY BOOK OF MAMMOTH PIKE, FRED BULLER

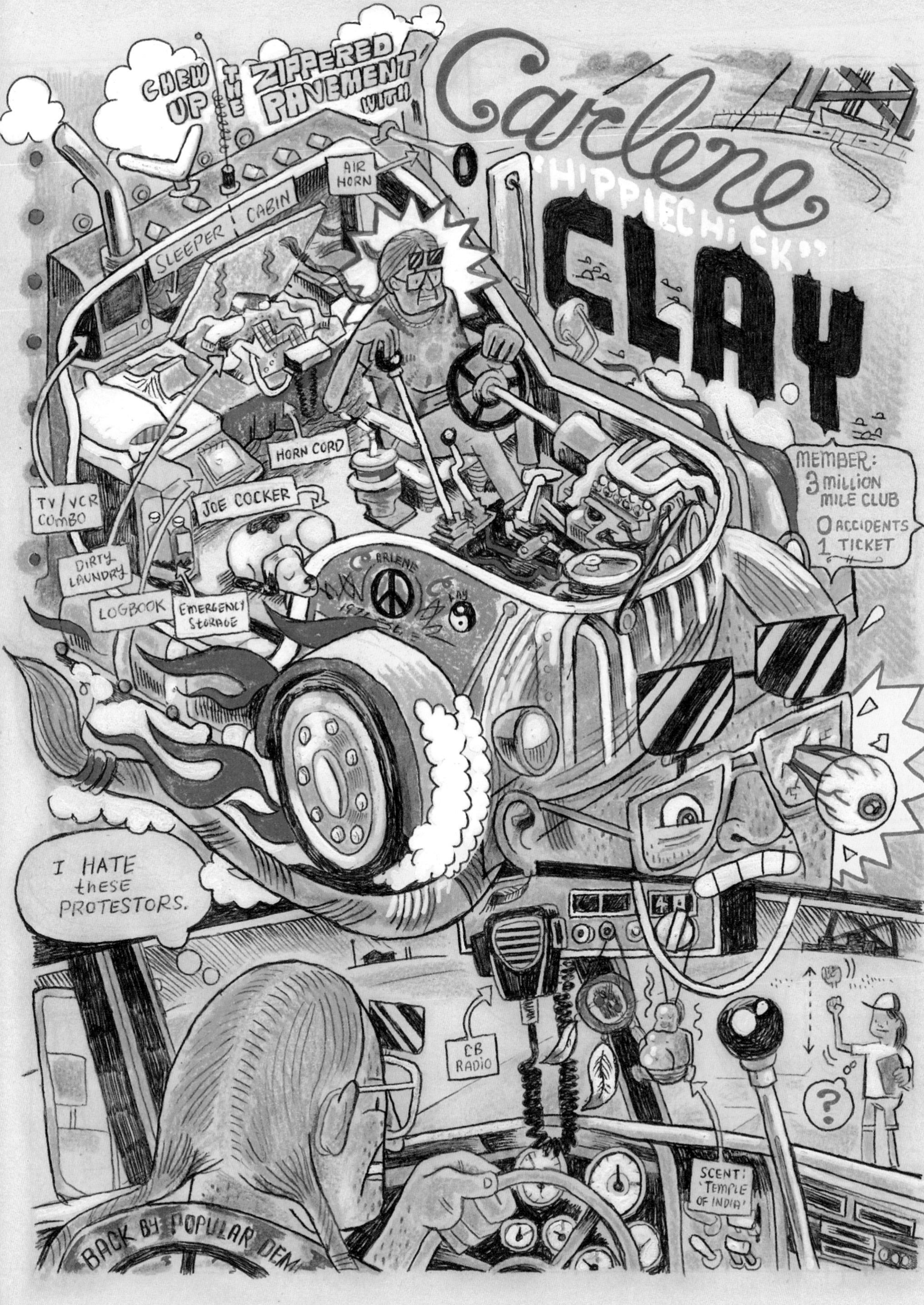
CHEW UP THE ZIPPERED PAVEMENT WITH
Carlene
"HIPPIECHICK"
CLAY
AIR HORN
SLEEPER
CABIN
HORN CORD
TV/VCR COMBO
JOE COCKER
DIRTY LAUNDRY
LOGBOOK
EMERGENCY STORAGE
MEMBER: 3 MILLION MILE CLUB
0 ACCIDENTS
1 TICKET
I HATE these PROTESTORS.
CB RADIO
SCENT: 'TEMPLE OF INDIA'
BACK BY POPULAR DEM

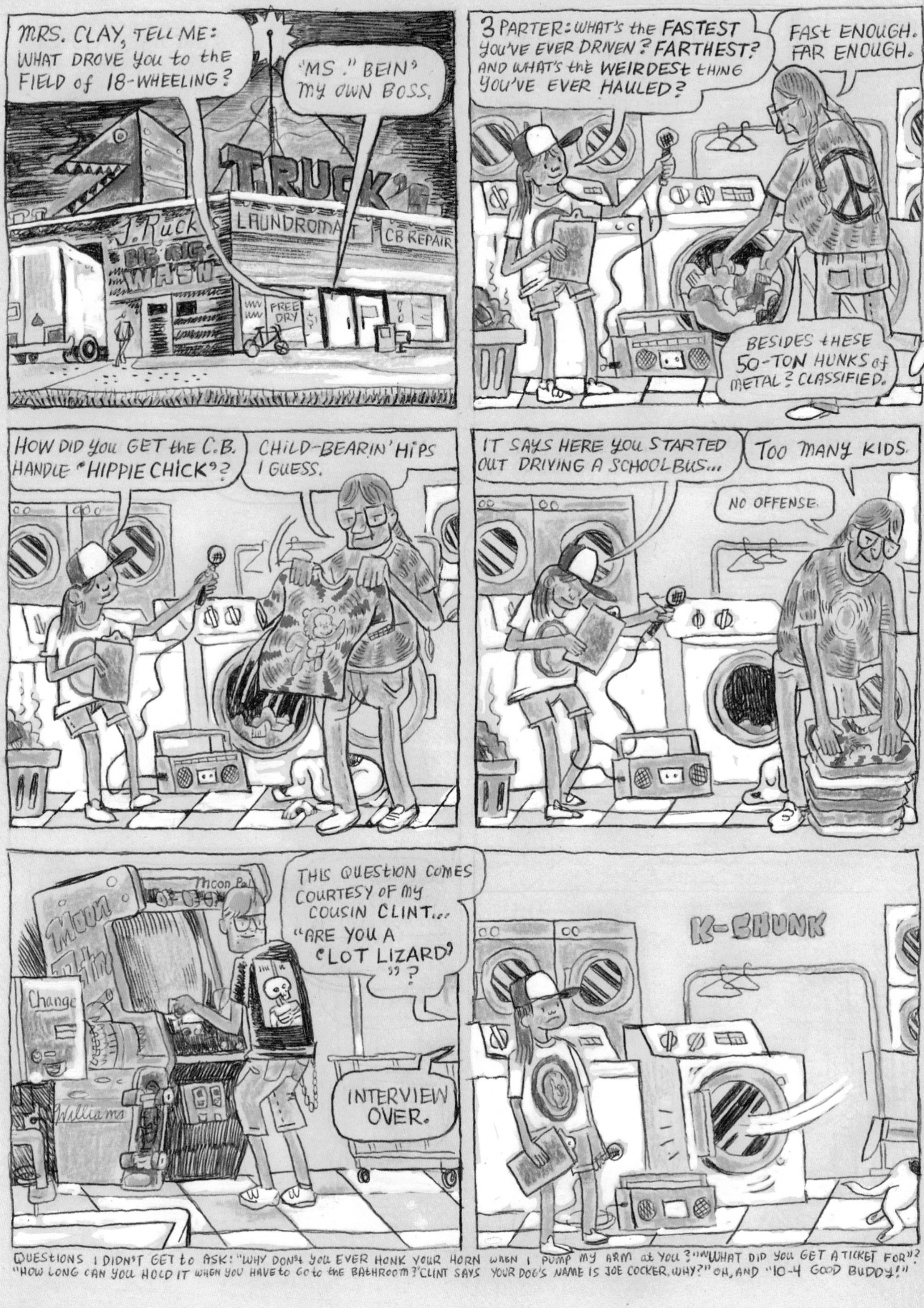
MRS. CLAY, TELL ME: WHAT DROVE YOU TO THE FIELD OF 18-WHEELING?
"MS." BEIN' MY OWN BOSS.
TRUCK'S
J. RUCK'S BIG RIG WASH
LAUNDROMAT
CB REPAIR
FREE DRY
3 PARTER: WHAT'S THE FASTEST YOU'VE EVER DRIVEN? FARTHEST? AND WHAT'S THE WEIRDEST THING YOU'VE EVER HAULED?
FAST ENOUGH. FAR ENOUGH.
BESIDES THESE 50-TON HUNKS OF METAL? CLASSIFIED.
HOW DID YOU GET THE C.B. HANDLE "HIPPIE CHICK"?
CHILD-BEARIN' HIPS I GUESS.
IT SAYS HERE YOU STARTED OUT DRIVING A SCHOOLBUS...
TOO MANY KIDS.
NO OFFENSE.
Moon Pal
Change
Williams
THIS QUESTION COMES COURTESY OF MY COUSIN CLINT... "ARE YOU A "LOT LIZARD""?
INTERVIEW OVER.
K-CHUNK

QUESTIONS I DIDN'T GET TO ASK: "WHY DON'T YOU EVER HONK YOUR HORN WHEN I PUMP MY ARM AT YOU?" "WHAT DID YOU GET A TICKET FOR"? "HOW LONG CAN YOU HOLD IT WHEN YOU HAVE TO GO TO THE BATHROOM?" CLINT SAYS YOUR DOG'S NAME IS JOE COCKER, WHY?" OH, AND "10-4 GOOD BUDDY!"

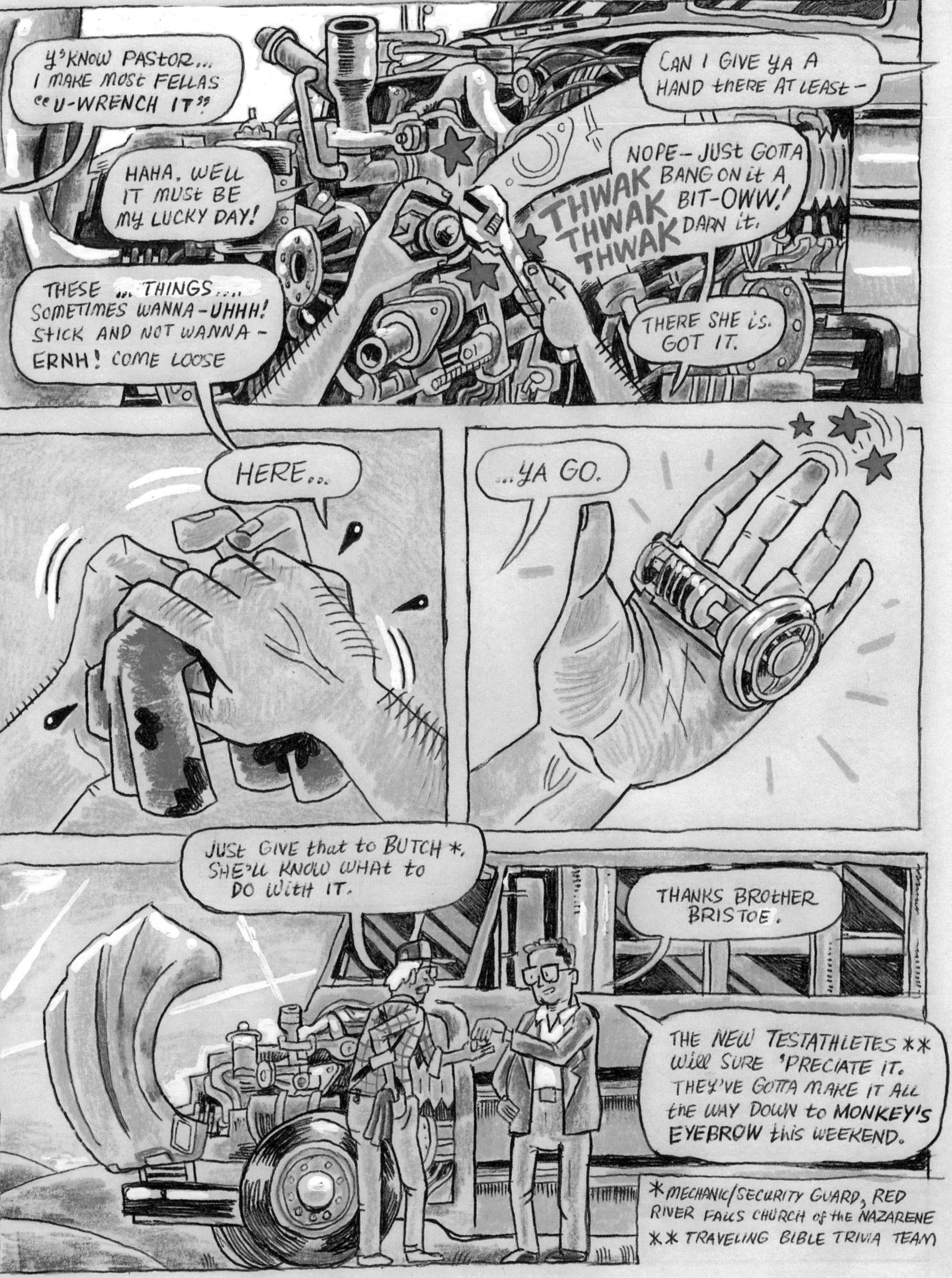
Y'KNOW PASTOR... I MAKE MOST FELLAS "U-WRENCH IT"
HAHA, WELL IT MUST BE MY LUCKY DAY!
THESE ... THINGS.... SOMETIMES WANNA-UHHH! STICK AND NOT WANNA - ERNH! COME LOOSE
CAN I GIVE YA A HAND THERE AT LEAST -
NOPE - JUST GOTTA BANG ON IT A BIT - OWW! DARN IT.
THWAK THWAK THWAK
THERE SHE IS. GOT IT.
HERE...
...YA GO.
JUST GIVE THAT TO BUTCH *. SHE'LL KNOW WHAT TO DO WITH IT.
THANKS BROTHER BRISTOE.
THE NEW TESTATHLETES ** WILL SURE 'PRECIATE IT. THEY'VE GOTTA MAKE IT ALL THE WAY DOWN TO MONKEY'S EYEBROW THIS WEEKEND.
* MECHANIC/SECURITY GUARD, RED RIVER FALLS CHURCH OF THE NAZARENE
** TRAVELING BIBLE TRIVIA TEAM

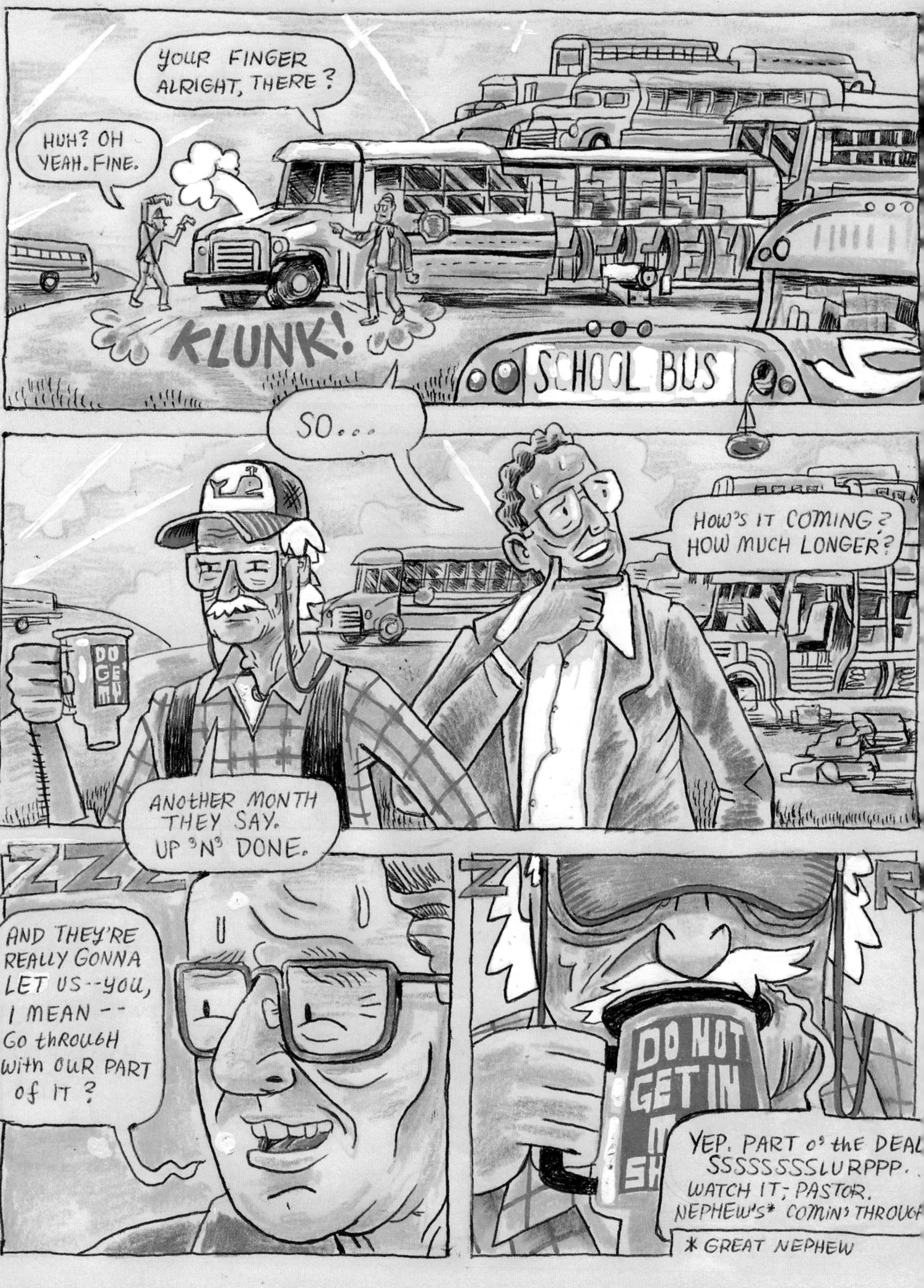
YOUR FINGER ALRIGHT, THERE?
HUH? OH YEAH. FINE.
KLUNK!
SCHOOL BUS
SO...
HOW'S IT COMING? HOW MUCH LONGER?
ANOTHER MONTH THEY SAY. UP 'N' DONE.
ZZZ
AND THEY'RE REALLY GONNA LET US--YOU, I MEAN-- GO THROUGH WITH OUR PART OF IT?
Z
DO NOT GET IN
YEP. PART O' THE DEAL
SSSSSSSSLURPPP.
WATCH IT, PASTOR. NEPHEW'S* COMIN' THROUGH
* GREAT NEPHEW

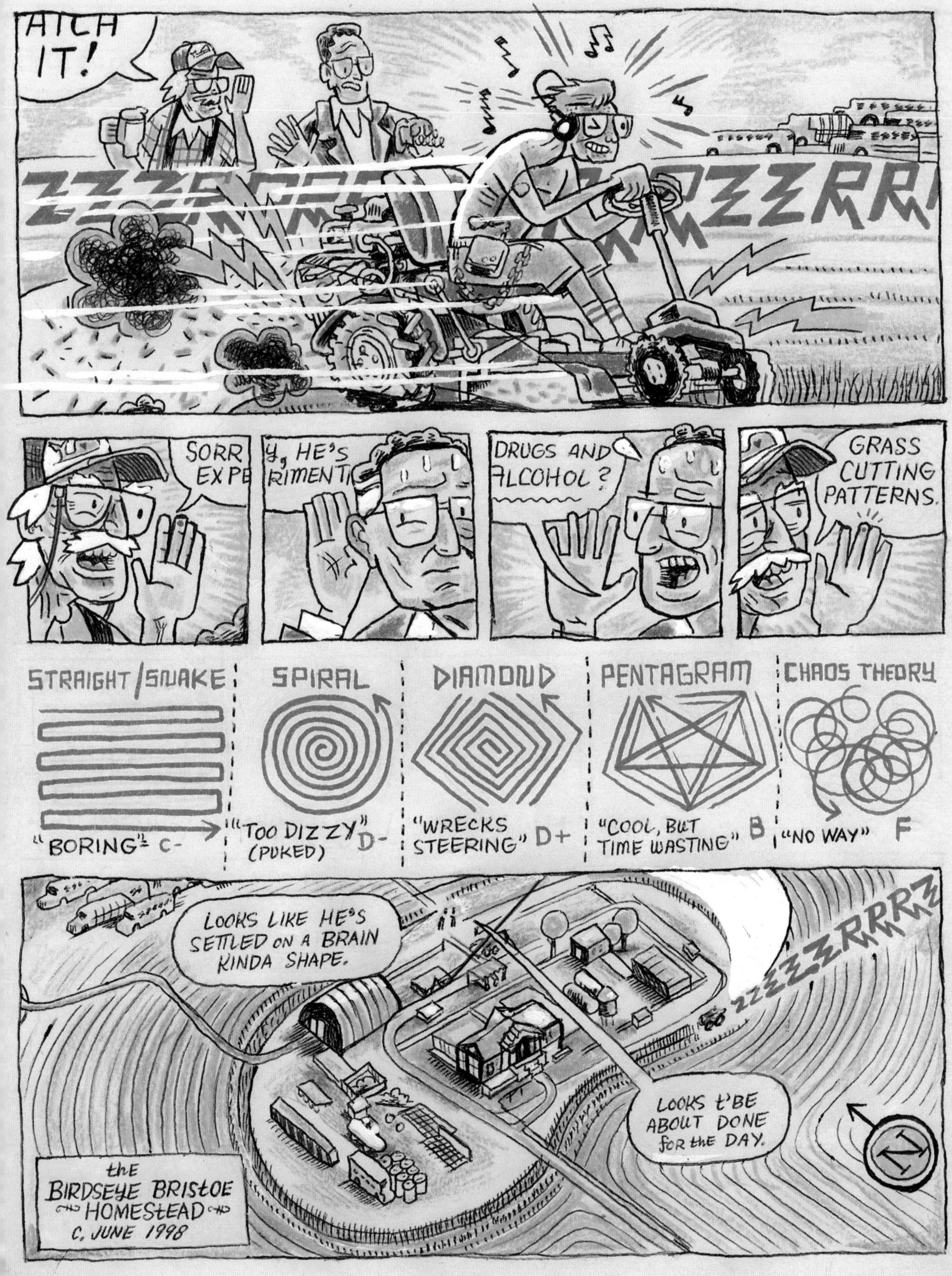
ATCH IT!
SORR EXPE
Y, HE'S RIMENT
DRUGS AND ALCOHOL?
GRASS CUTTING PATTERNS.
STRAIGHT/SNAKE
"BORING" C-
SPIRAL
"TOO DIZZY" (PUKED) D-
DIAMOND
"WRECKS STEERING" D+
PENTAGRAM
"COOL, BUT TIME WASTING" B
CHAOS THEORY
"NO WAY" F
LOOKS LIKE HE'S SETTLED ON A BRAIN KINDA SHAPE.
LOOKS t'BE ABOUT DONE for the DAY.
the BIRDSEYE BRISTOE HOMESTEAD
C. JUNE 1998

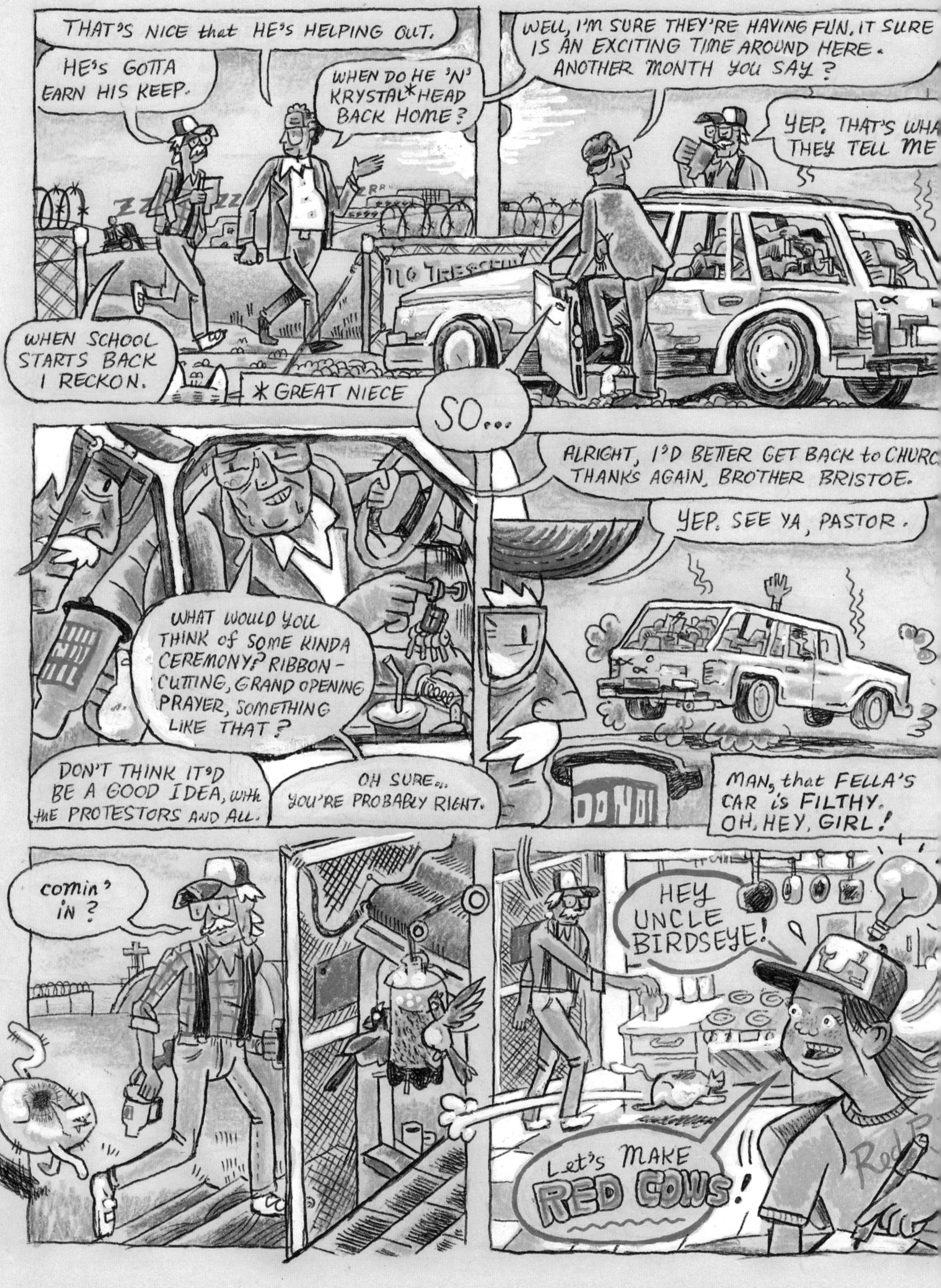
THAT'S NICE that HE'S HELPING OUT.
HE'S GOTTA EARN HIS KEEP.
WHEN DO HE 'N' KRYSTAL* HEAD BACK HOME?
WHEN SCHOOL STARTS BACK I RECKON.
NO TRESPASSING
* GREAT NIECE
WELL, I'M SURE THEY'RE HAVING FUN. IT SURE IS AN EXCITING TIME AROUND HERE. ANOTHER MONTH YOU SAY?
YEP. THAT'S WHA THEY TELL ME
SO...
WHAT WOULD YOU THINK of SOME KINDA CEREMONY? RIBBON-CUTTING, GRAND OPENING PRAYER, SOMETHING LIKE THAT?
DON'T THINK IT'D BE A GOOD IDEA, with the PROTESTORS AND ALL.
OH SURE... YOU'RE PROBABLY RIGHT.
ALRIGHT, I'D BETTER GET BACK to CHURC THANKS AGAIN, BROTHER BRISTOE.
YEP. SEE YA, PASTOR.
MAN, that FELLA'S CAR is FILTHY. OH, HEY, GIRL!
comin' in?
HEY UNCLE BIRDSEYE!
Let's MAKE RED COWS!

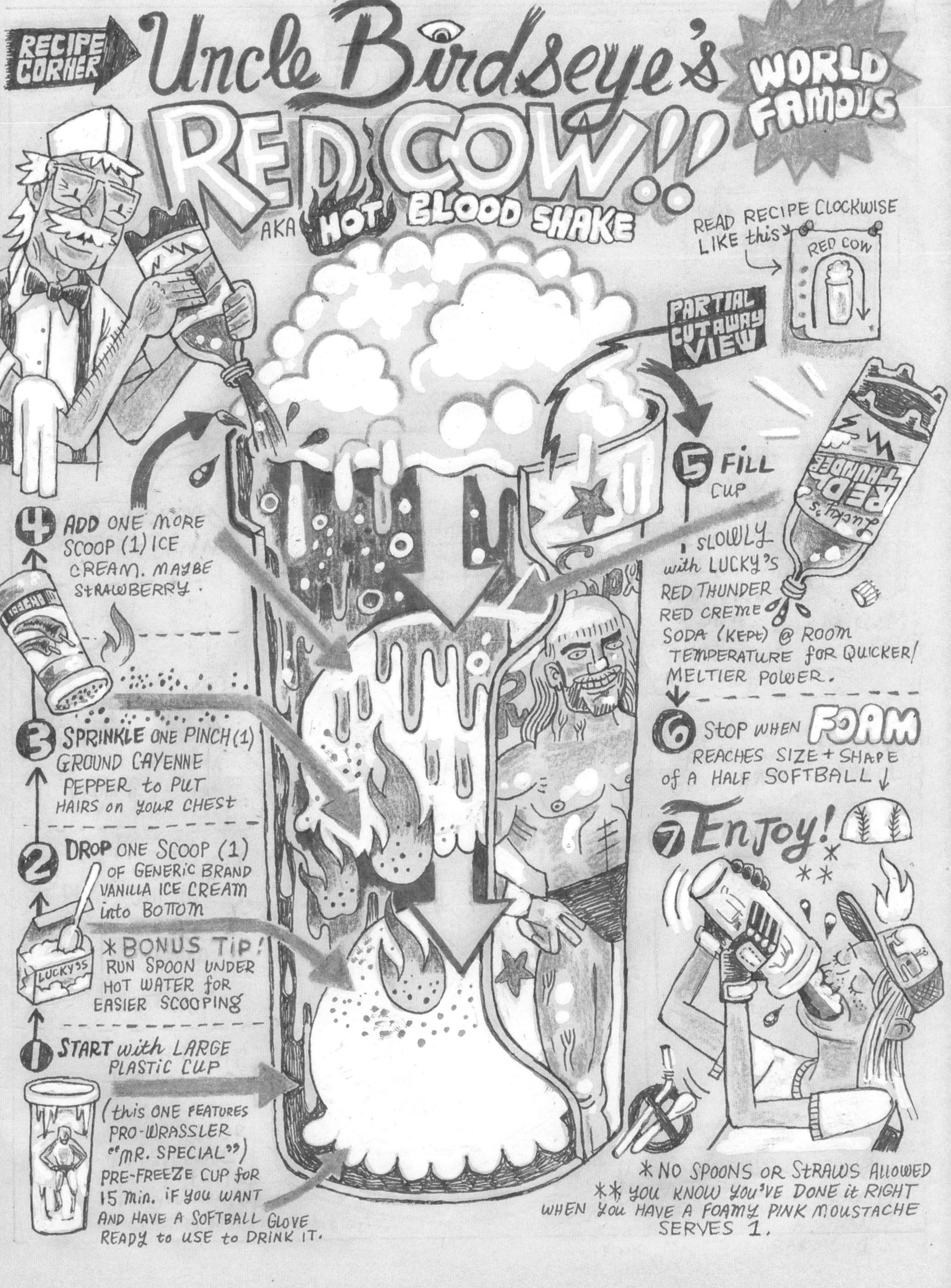
RECIPE CORNER
Uncle Birdseye's
WORLD FAMOUS
RED COW!!
AKA HOT BLOOD SHAKE
READ RECIPE CLOCKWISE LIKE this
RED COW
PARTIAL CUTAWAY VIEW
1 START with LARGE PLASTIC CUP
(this ONE FEATURES PRO-WRASSLER "MR. SPECIAL") PRE-FREEZE CUP for 15 min. if you WANT AND HAVE A SOFTBALL GLOVE READY to USE to DRINK IT.
2 DROP ONE SCOOP (1) OF GENERIC BRAND VANILLA ICE CREAM into BOTTOM
LUCKY'S
*BONUS TIP! RUN SPOON UNDER HOT WATER for EASIER SCOOPING
3 SPRINKLE ONE PINCH (1) GROUND CAYENNE PEPPER to PUT HAIRS on YOUR CHEST
4 ADD ONE MORE SCOOP (1) ICE CREAM. MAYBE STRAWBERRY.
5 FILL CUP
SLOWLY with LUCKY'S RED THUNDER RED CREME SODA (KEPT) @ ROOM TEMPERATURE for QUICKER/MELTIER POWER.
Lucky's RED THUNDER
6 STOP WHEN FOAM REACHES SIZE + SHAPE of A HALF SOFTBALL
7 Enjoy!
* NO SPOONS OR STRAWS ALLOWED
** YOU KNOW YOU'VE DONE IT RIGHT WHEN YOU HAVE A FOAMY PINK MOUSTACHE
SERVES 1.

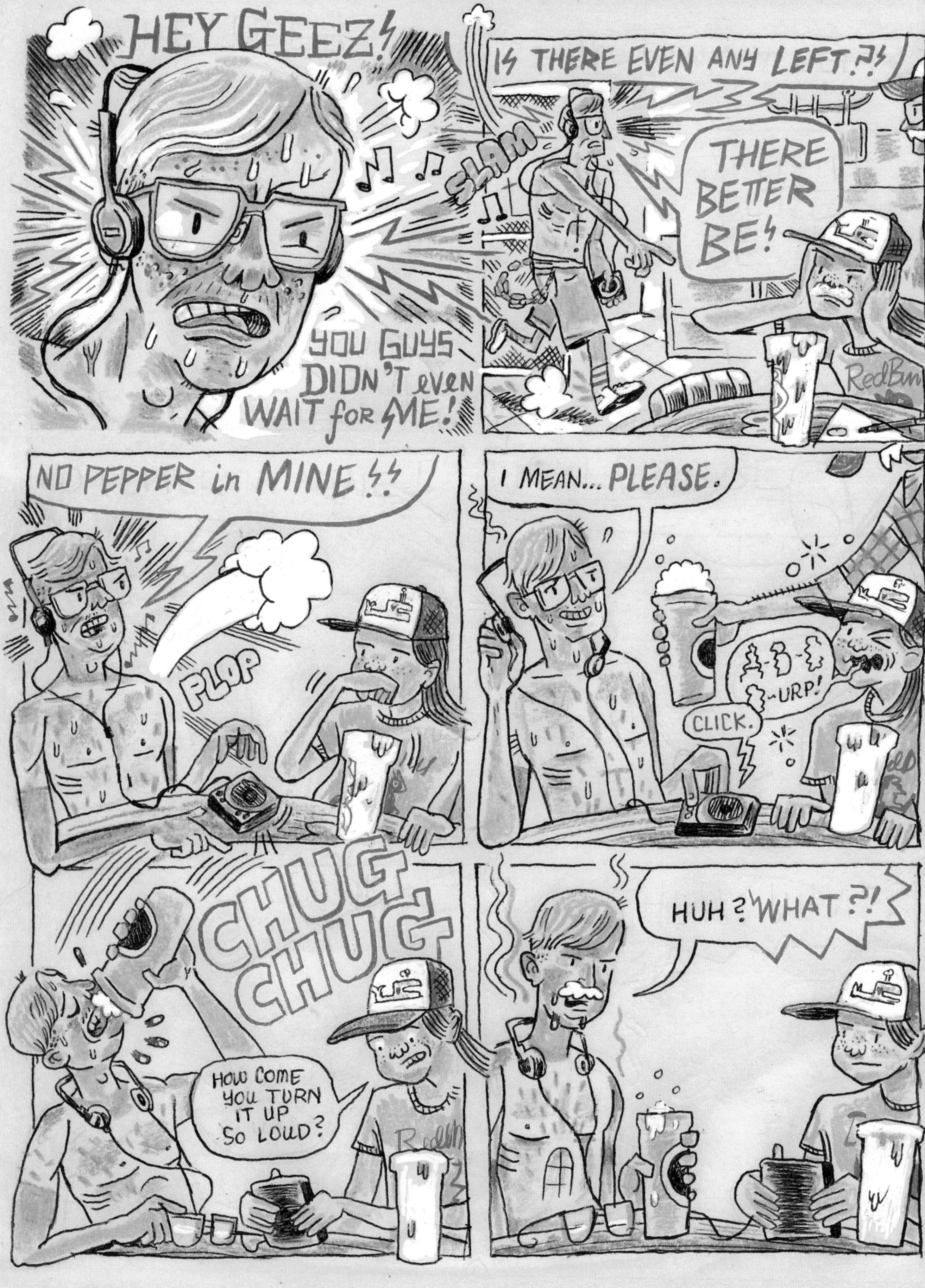
HEY GEEZ!
YOU GUYS DIDN'T even WAIT for ME!
SLAM
IS THERE EVEN ANY LEFT?!
THERE BETTER BE!
NO PEPPER in MINE?!
PLOP
I MEAN... PLEASE.
CLICK.
~URP!
CHUG CHUG
HOW COME YOU TURN IT UP SO LOUD?
HUH? WHAT?!

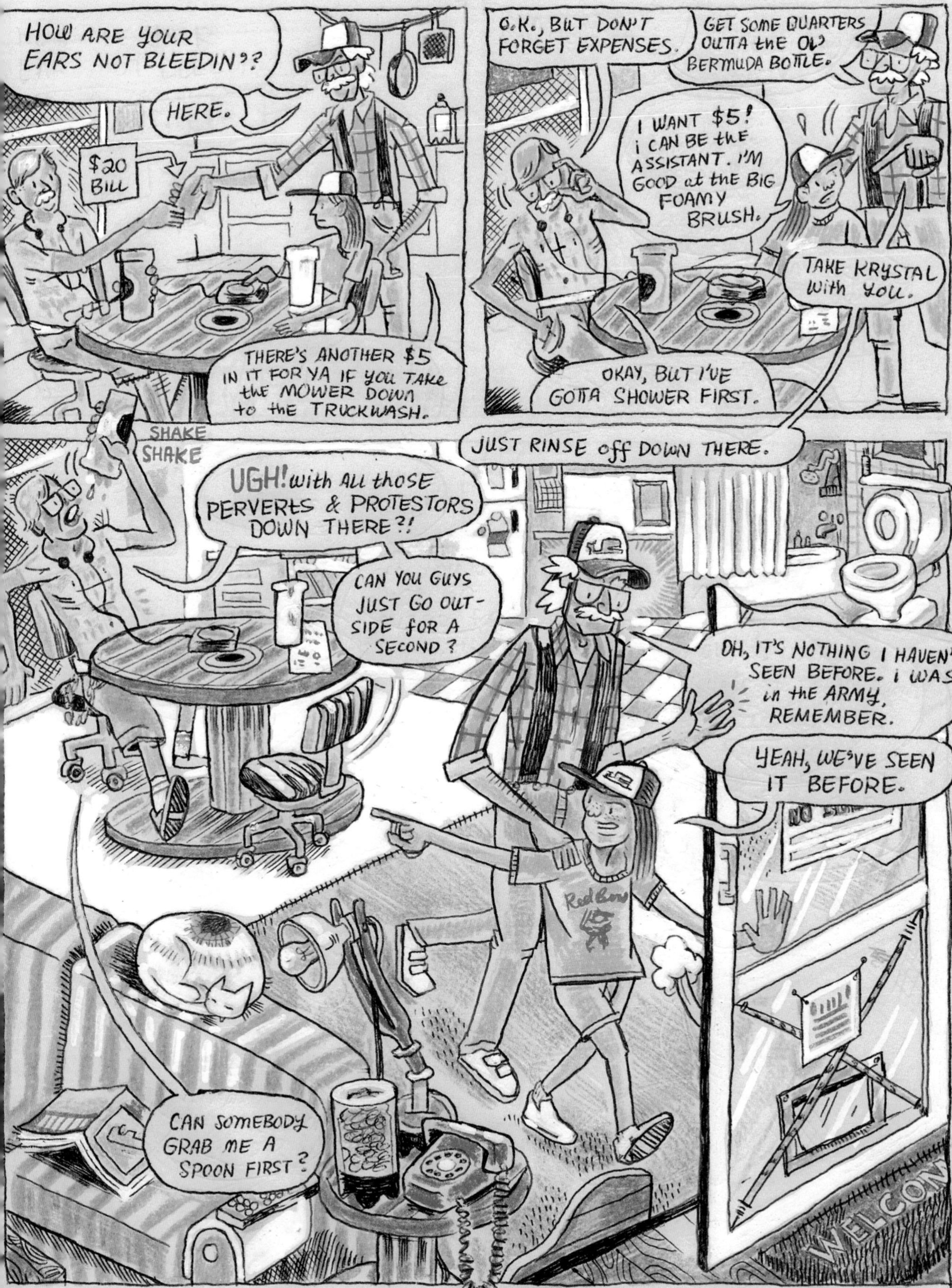
HOW ARE YOUR EARS NOT BLEEDIN'?
HERE.
$20 BILL
THERE'S ANOTHER $5 IN IT FOR YA IF YOU TAKE THE MOWER DOWN TO THE TRUCKWASH.
O.K., BUT DON'T FORGET EXPENSES.
GET SOME QUARTERS OUTTA THE OL' BERMUDA BOTTLE.
I WANT $5! I CAN BE THE ASSISTANT. I'M GOOD AT THE BIG FOAMY BRUSH.
TAKE KRYSTAL WITH YOU.
OKAY, BUT I'VE GOTTA SHOWER FIRST.
JUST RINSE OFF DOWN THERE.
SHAKE SHAKE
UGH! WITH ALL THOSE PERVERTS & PROTESTORS DOWN THERE?!
CAN YOU GUYS JUST GO OUTSIDE FOR A SECOND?
OH, IT'S NOTHING I HAVEN'T SEEN BEFORE. I WAS IN THE ARMY, REMEMBER.
YEAH, WE'VE SEEN IT BEFORE.
CAN SOMEBODY GRAB ME A SPOON FIRST?
WELCOM

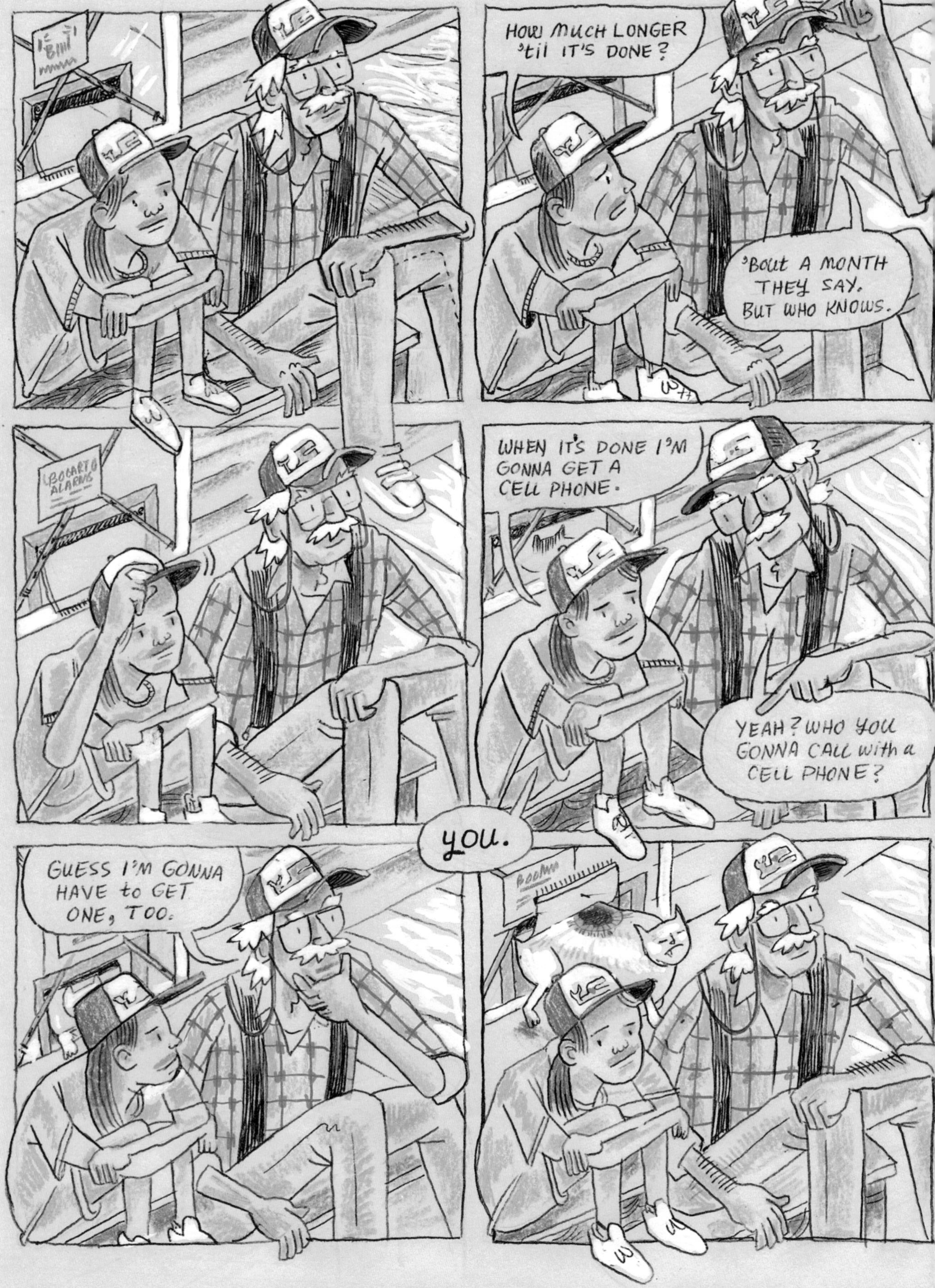
HOW MUCH LONGER 'til IT'S DONE?
'BOUT A MONTH THEY SAY. BUT WHO KNOWS.
BOGART ALARMS
WHEN IT'S DONE I'M GONNA GET A CELL PHONE.
YEAH? WHO YOU GONNA CALL with a CELL PHONE?
you.
GUESS I'M GONNA HAVE to GET ONE, TOO.

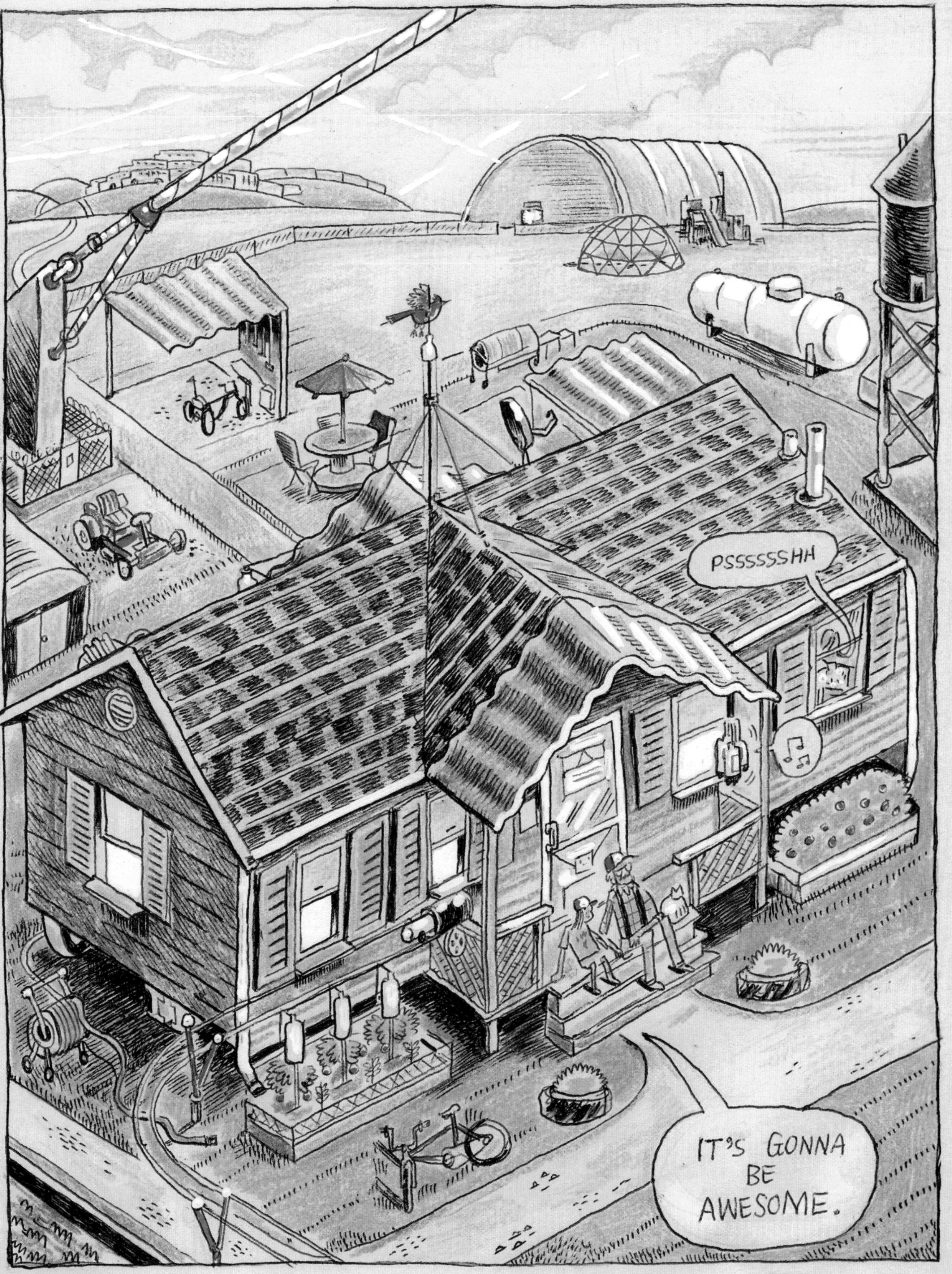
PSSSSSSHH
IT'S GONNA BE AWESOME.

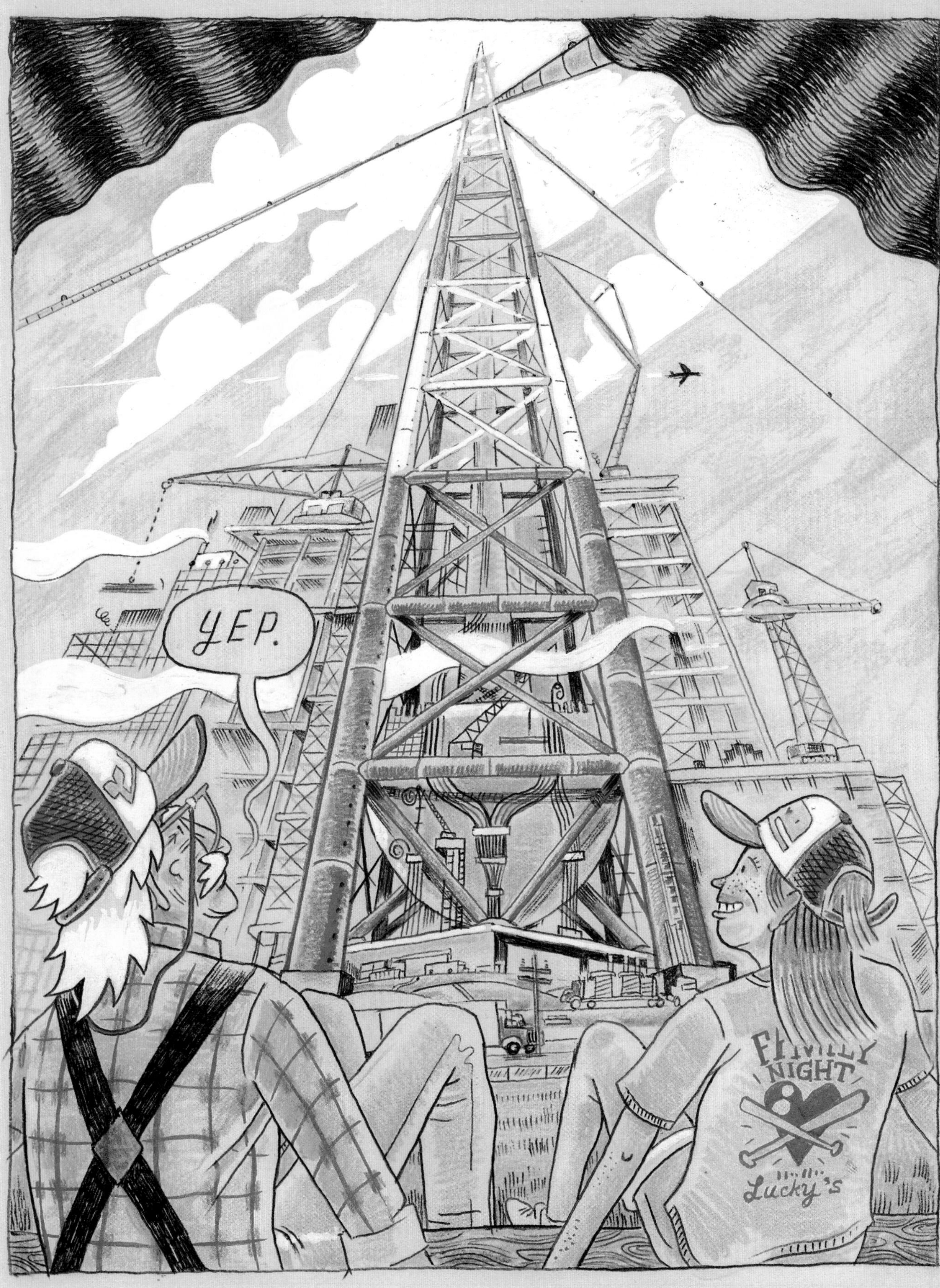
YEP.
NIGHT
Lucky's

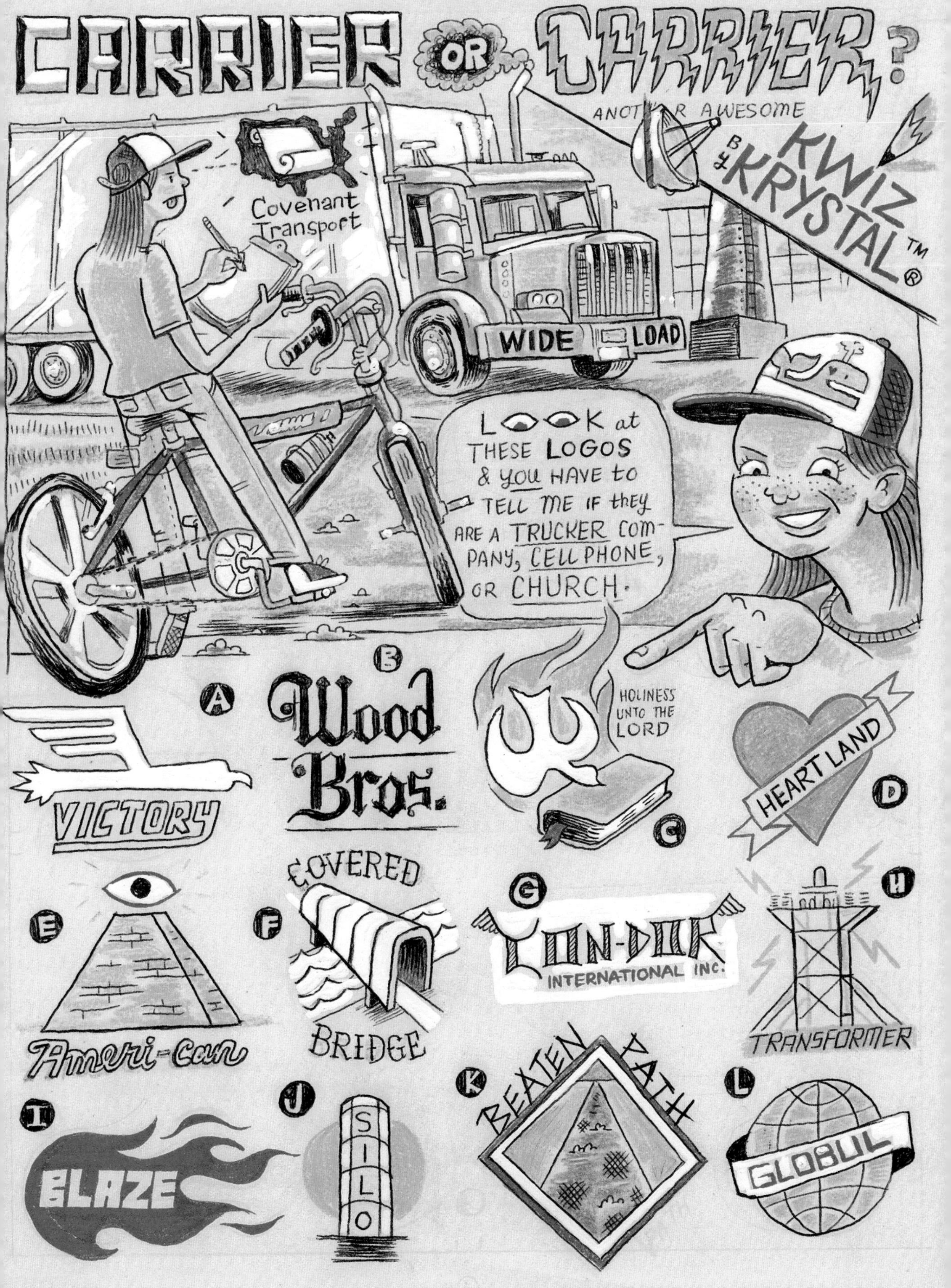
CARRIER OR CARRIER?
ANOTHER AWESOME KWIZ BY KRYSTAL™®
Covenant Transport
WIDE LOAD
LOOK at THESE LOGOS & YOU HAVE to TELL ME IF they ARE A TRUCKER COMPANY, CELL PHONE, OR CHURCH.
A VICTORY
B Wood Bros.
C HOLINESS UNTO THE LORD
D HEARTLAND
E Ameri-can
F COVERED BRIDGE
G CON-DOR INTERNATIONAL INC.
H TRANSFORMER
I BLAZE
J SILO
K BEATEN PATH
L GLOBUL

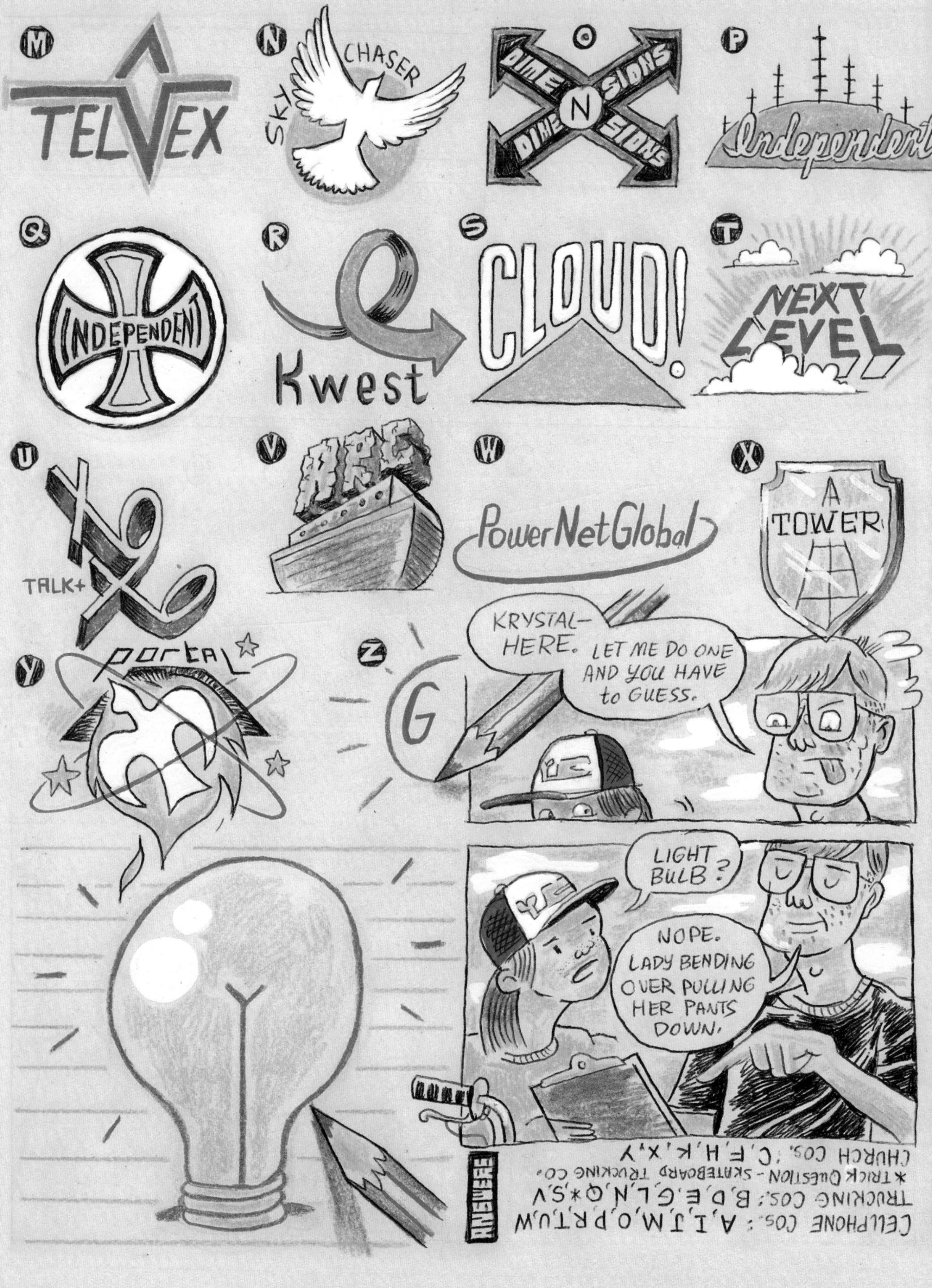

M
TELVEX
N
SKY CHASER
O
DIMENSIONS
N
DIMENSIONS
P
Independent
Q
INDEPENDENT
R
Kwest
S
CLOUD!
T
NEXT LEVEL
U
TALK+
V
ARC
W
PowerNetGlobal
X
A TOWER
Y
portal
Z
G
KRYSTAL- HERE.
LET ME DO ONE AND YOU HAVE to GUESS.
LIGHT BULB?
NOPE. LADY BENDING OVER PULLING HER PANTS DOWN.
ANSWERS
CELLPHONE COS: A, I, J, M, O, P, R, T, U, W
TRUCKING COS: B, D, E, G, L, N, Q*, S, V
*TRICK QUESTION - SKATEBOARD TRUCKING CO.
CHURCH COS: C, F, H, K, X, Y

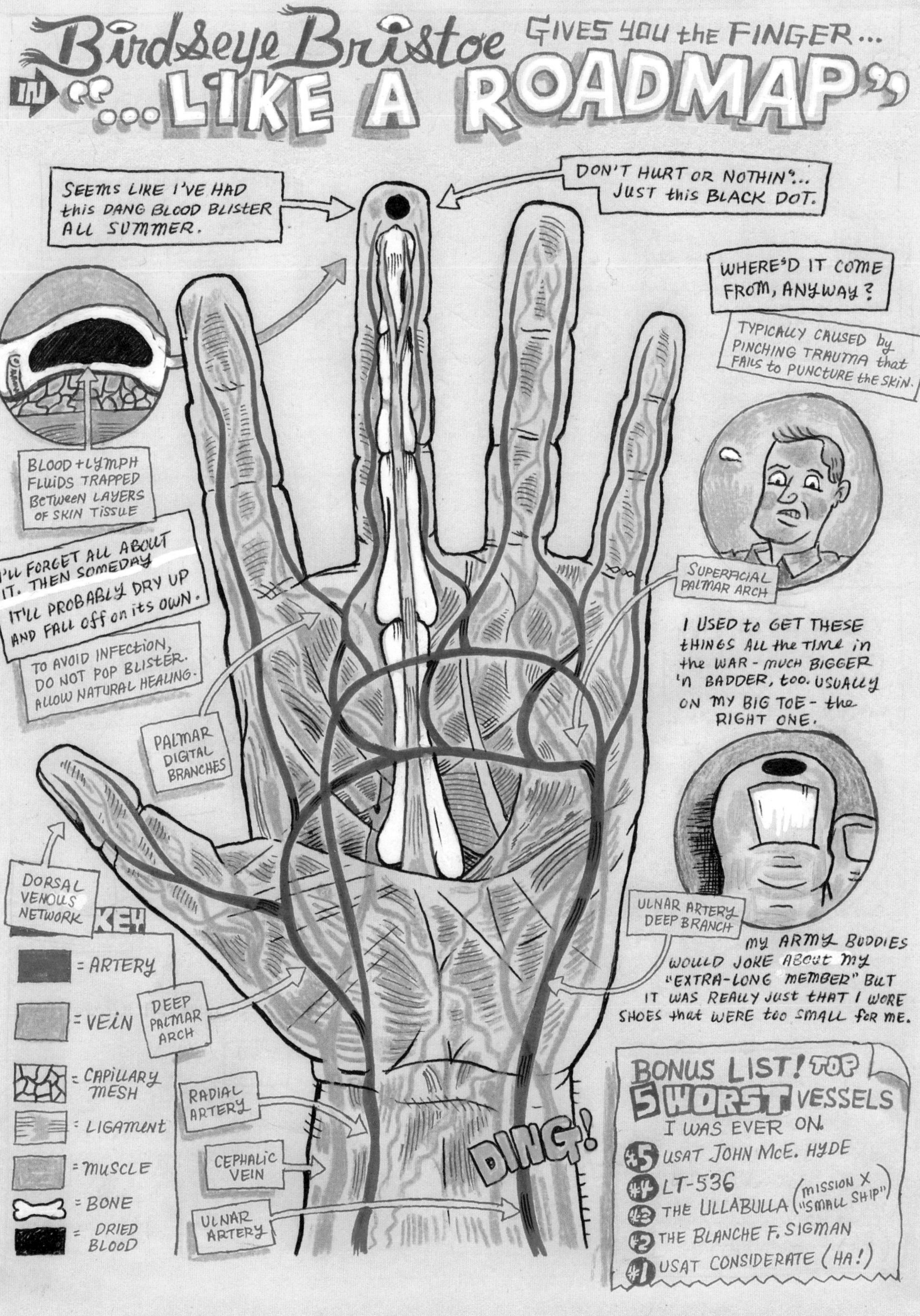

Birdseye Bristoe GIVES YOU THE FINGER...
IN "...LIKE A ROADMAP"
SEEMS LIKE I'VE HAD this DANG BLOOD BLISTER ALL SUMMER.
DON'T HURT OR NOTHIN'... JUST this BLACK DOT.
WHERE'D IT COME FROM, ANYWAY?
TYPICALLY CAUSED by PINCHING TRAUMA that FAILS to PUNCTURE the SKIN.
BLOOD + LYMPH FLUIDS TRAPPED BETWEEN LAYERS OF SKIN TISSUE
I'LL FORGET ALL ABOUT IT. THEN SOMEDAY IT'LL PROBABLY DRY UP AND FALL OFF on its OWN.
TO AVOID INFECTION, DO NOT POP BLISTER. ALLOW NATURAL HEALING.
SUPERFACIAL PALMAR ARCH
I USED to GET THESE things ALL the TIME in the WAR - MUCH BIGGER 'N BADDER, too. USUALLY ON MY BIG TOE - the RIGHT ONE.
PALMAR DIGITAL BRANCHES
DORSAL VENOUS NETWORK
KEY
= ARTERY
= VEIN
= CAPILLARY MESH
= LIGAMENT
= MUSCLE
= BONE
= DRIED BLOOD
ULNAR ARTERY DEEP BRANCH
MY ARMY BUDDIES WOULD JOKE ABOUT MY "EXTRA-LONG MEMBER" BUT IT WAS REALLY JUST THAT I WORE SHOES that WERE too SMALL for ME.
DEEP PALMAR ARCH
RADIAL ARTERY
CEPHALIC VEIN
ULNAR ARTERY
DING!
BONUS LIST! TOP 5 WORST VESSELS I WAS EVER ON.
#5 USAT JOHN McE. HYDE
#4 LT-536
#3 THE ULLABULLA (MISSION X "SMALL SHIP")
#2 THE BLANCHE F. SIGMAN
#1 USAT CONSIDERATE (HA!)

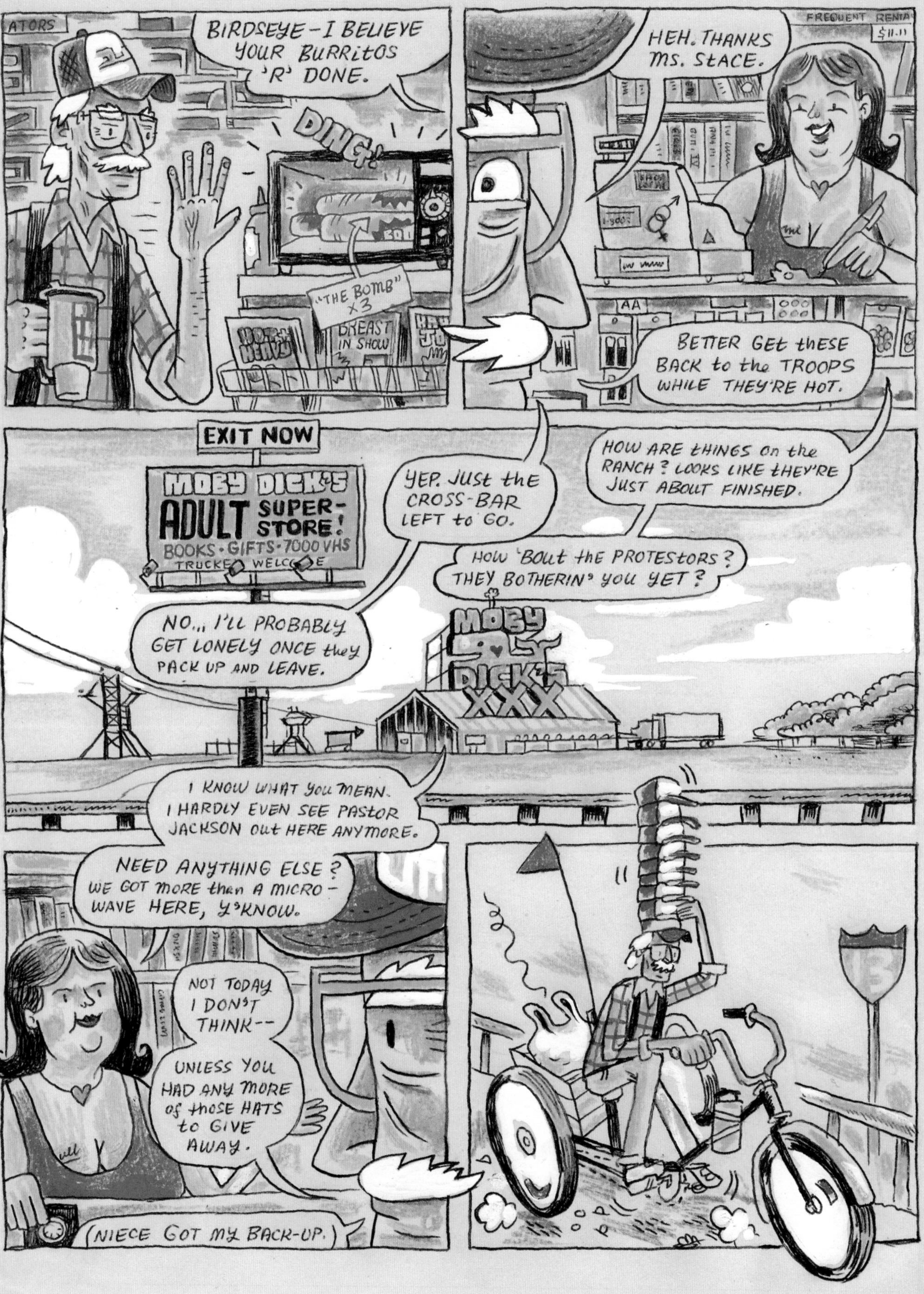
ATORS
BIRDSEYE - I BELIEVE YOUR BURRITOS 'R' DONE.
DING!
"THE BOMB" x3
BREAST IN SHOW
FREQUENT RENTA
$11.11
HEH. THANKS MS. STACE.
BETTER GET THESE BACK TO THE TROOPS WHILE THEY'RE HOT.
EXIT NOW
MOBY DICK'S ADULT SUPER-STORE!
BOOKS • GIFTS • 7000 VHS
HOW ARE THINGS ON THE RANCH? LOOKS LIKE THEY'RE JUST ABOUT FINISHED.
YEP. JUST THE CROSS-BAR LEFT TO GO.
HOW 'BOUT THE PROTESTORS? THEY BOTHERIN' YOU YET?
NO... I'LL PROBABLY GET LONELY ONCE THEY PACK UP AND LEAVE.
MOBY DICK'S XXX
I KNOW WHAT YOU MEAN. I HARDLY EVEN SEE PASTOR JACKSON OUT HERE ANYMORE.
NEED ANYTHING ELSE? WE GOT MORE THAN A MICRO-WAVE HERE, Y'KNOW.
NOT TODAY I DON'T THINK--
UNLESS YOU HAD ANY MORE OF THOSE HATS TO GIVE AWAY.
(NIECE GOT MY BACK-UP.)

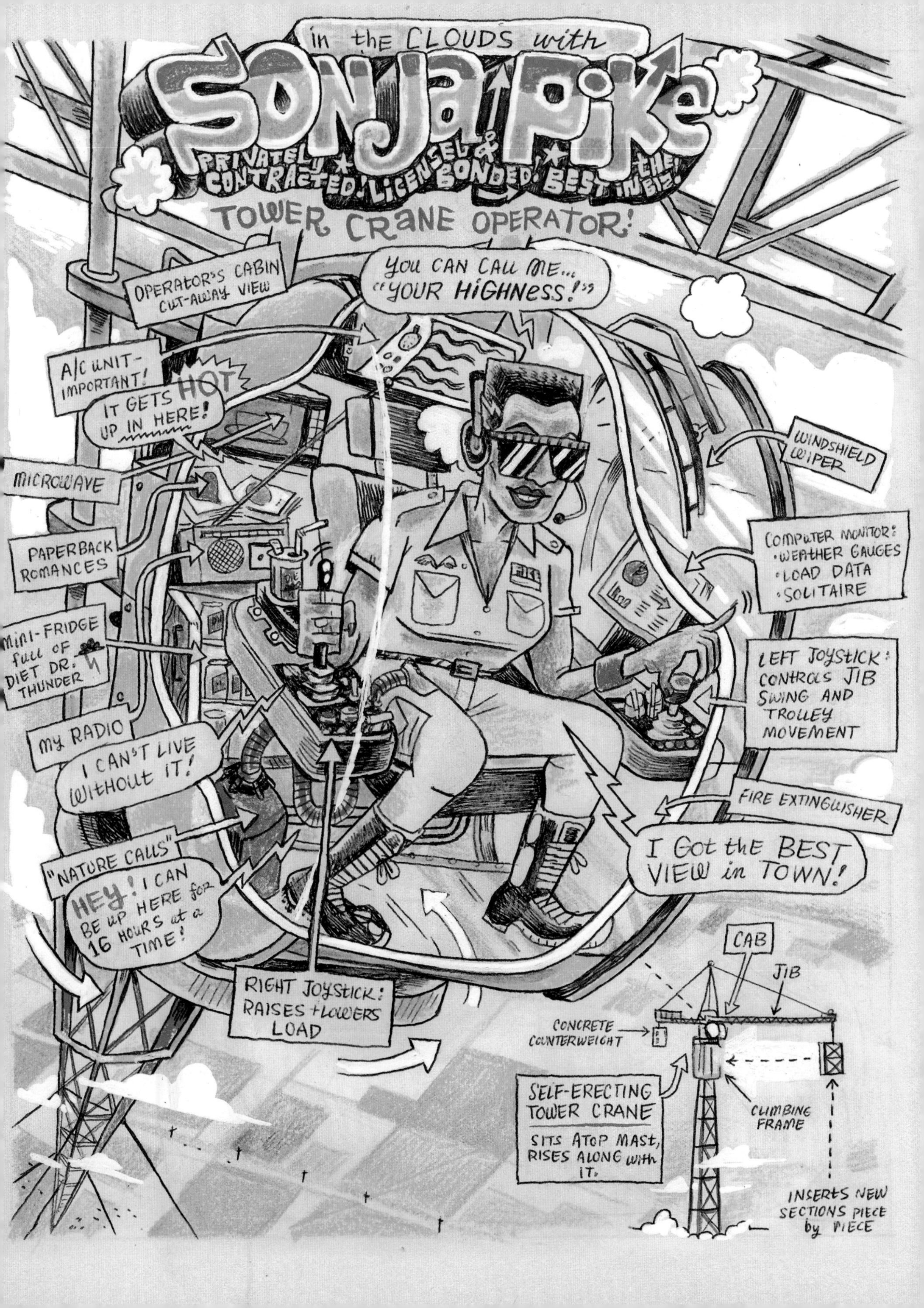
in the CLOUDS with
SONJA PIKE
PRIVATELY ★ CONTRACTED! LICENSED & BONDED! ★ THE BEST IN BIZ!
TOWER CRANE OPERATOR!
OPERATOR'S CABIN CUT-AWAY VIEW
YOU CAN CALL ME... "YOUR HIGHNESS!"
A/C UNIT- IMPORTANT!
IT GETS HOT UP IN HERE!
MICROWAVE
PAPERBACK ROMANCES
MINI-FRIDGE full of DIET DR. THUNDER
MY RADIO
I CAN'T LIVE WITHOUT IT!
"NATURE CALLS"
HEY! I CAN BE UP HERE for 16 HOURS at a TIME!
WINDSHIELD WIPER
COMPUTER MONITOR: •WEATHER GAUGES •LOAD DATA •SOLITAIRE
LEFT JOYSTICK: CONTROLS JIB SWING AND TROLLEY MOVEMENT
FIRE EXTINGUISHER
I Got the BEST VIEW in TOWN!
RIGHT JOYSTICK: RAISES + LOWERS LOAD
CAB
JIB
CONCRETE COUNTERWEIGHT
SELF-ERECTING TOWER CRANE
SITS ATOP MAST, RISES ALONG WITH IT.
CLIMBING FRAME
INSERTS NEW SECTIONS PIECE by PIECE

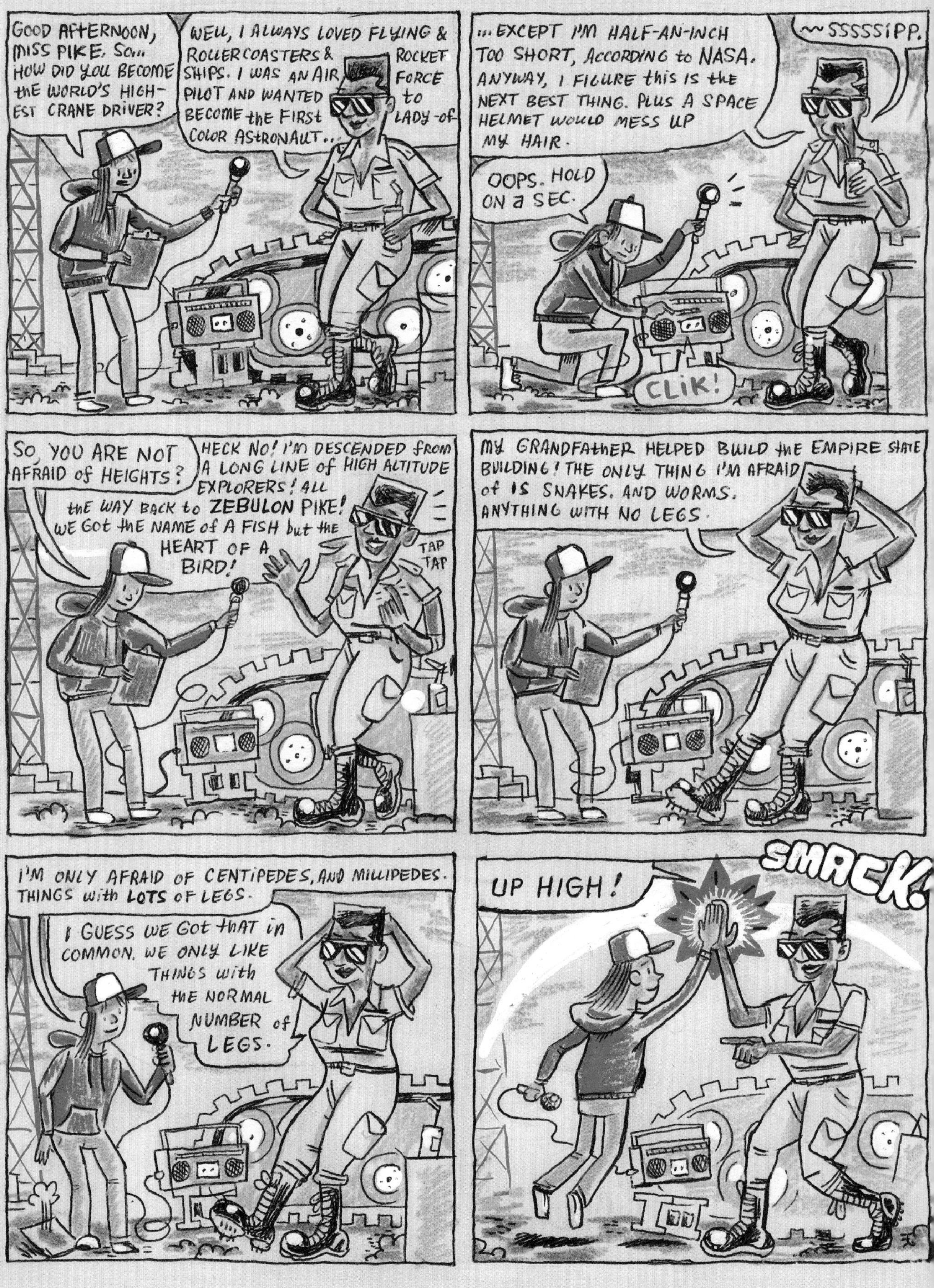

GOOD AFTERNOON, MISS PIKE. SO... HOW DID YOU BECOME THE WORLD'S HIGHEST CRANE DRIVER?
WELL, I ALWAYS LOVED FLYING & ROLLERCOASTERS & ROCKET SHIPS. I WAS AN AIR FORCE PILOT AND WANTED TO BECOME THE FIRST LADY-OF-COLOR ASTRONAUT...
...EXCEPT I'M HALF-AN-INCH TOO SHORT, ACCORDING TO NASA. ANYWAY, I FIGURE THIS IS THE NEXT BEST THING. PLUS A SPACE HELMET WOULD MESS UP MY HAIR.
~SSSSSIPP.
OOPS. HOLD ON A SEC.
CLIK!
SO, YOU ARE NOT AFRAID OF HEIGHTS?
HECK NO! I'M DESCENDED FROM A LONG LINE OF HIGH ALTITUDE EXPLORERS! ALL THE WAY BACK TO ZEBULON PIKE! WE GOT THE NAME OF A FISH BUT THE HEART OF A BIRD!
TAP TAP
MY GRANDFATHER HELPED BUILD THE EMPIRE STATE BUILDING! THE ONLY THING I'M AFRAID OF IS SNAKES. AND WORMS. ANYTHING WITH NO LEGS.
I'M ONLY AFRAID OF CENTIPEDES, AND MILLIPEDES. THINGS WITH LOTS OF LEGS.
I GUESS WE GOT THAT IN COMMON. WE ONLY LIKE THINGS WITH THE NORMAL NUMBER OF LEGS.
UP HIGH!
SMACK!

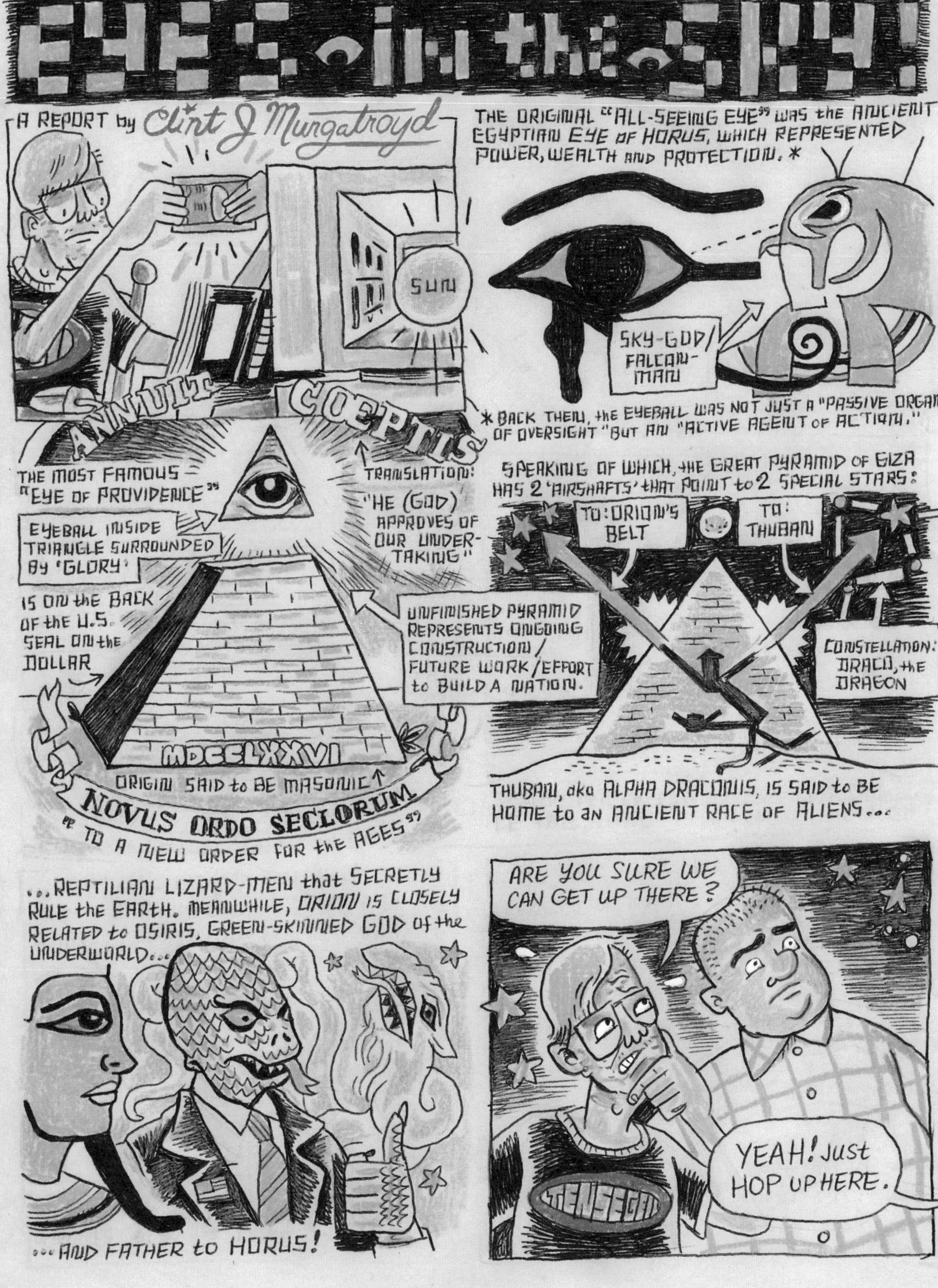
EYES in the SKY!
A REPORT by Clint J Murgatroyd
SUN
ANNUIT COEPTIS
THE ORIGINAL "ALL-SEEING EYE" WAS the ANCIENT EGYPTIAN EYE OF HORUS, WHICH REPRESENTED POWER, WEALTH AND PROTECTION. *
SKY-GOD/ FALCON-MAN
* BACK THEN, the EYEBALL WAS NOT JUST A "PASSIVE ORGAN OF OVERSIGHT" BUT AN "ACTIVE AGENT OF ACTION."
THE MOST FAMOUS "EYE OF PROVIDENCE"
EYEBALL INSIDE TRIANGLE SURROUNDED BY 'GLORY'
IS ON the BACK OF the U.S. SEAL ON the DOLLAR
TRANSLATION: 'HE (GOD) APPROVES OF OUR UNDERTAKING"
UNFINISHED PYRAMID REPRESENTS ONGOING CONSTRUCTION / FUTURE WORK/EFFORT to BUILD A NATION.
MDCCLXXVI
ORIGIN SAID to BE MASONIC
NOVUS ORDO SECLORUM
"TO A NEW ORDER FOR the AGES"
SPEAKING OF WHICH, the GREAT PYRAMID OF GIZA HAS 2 'AIRSHAFTS' THAT POINT to 2 SPECIAL STARS:
TO: ORION'S BELT
TO: THUBAN
CONSTELLATION: DRACO, the DRAGON
THUBAN, aka ALPHA DRACONIS, IS SAID to BE HOME to AN ANCIENT RACE OF ALIENS...
...REPTILIAN LIZARD-MEN that SECRETLY RULE the EARTH. MEANWHILE, ORION IS CLOSELY RELATED to OSIRIS, GREEN-SKINNED GOD of the UNDERWORLD...
...AND FATHER to HORUS!
ARE YOU SURE WE CAN GET UP THERE?
YEAH! Just HOP UP HERE.

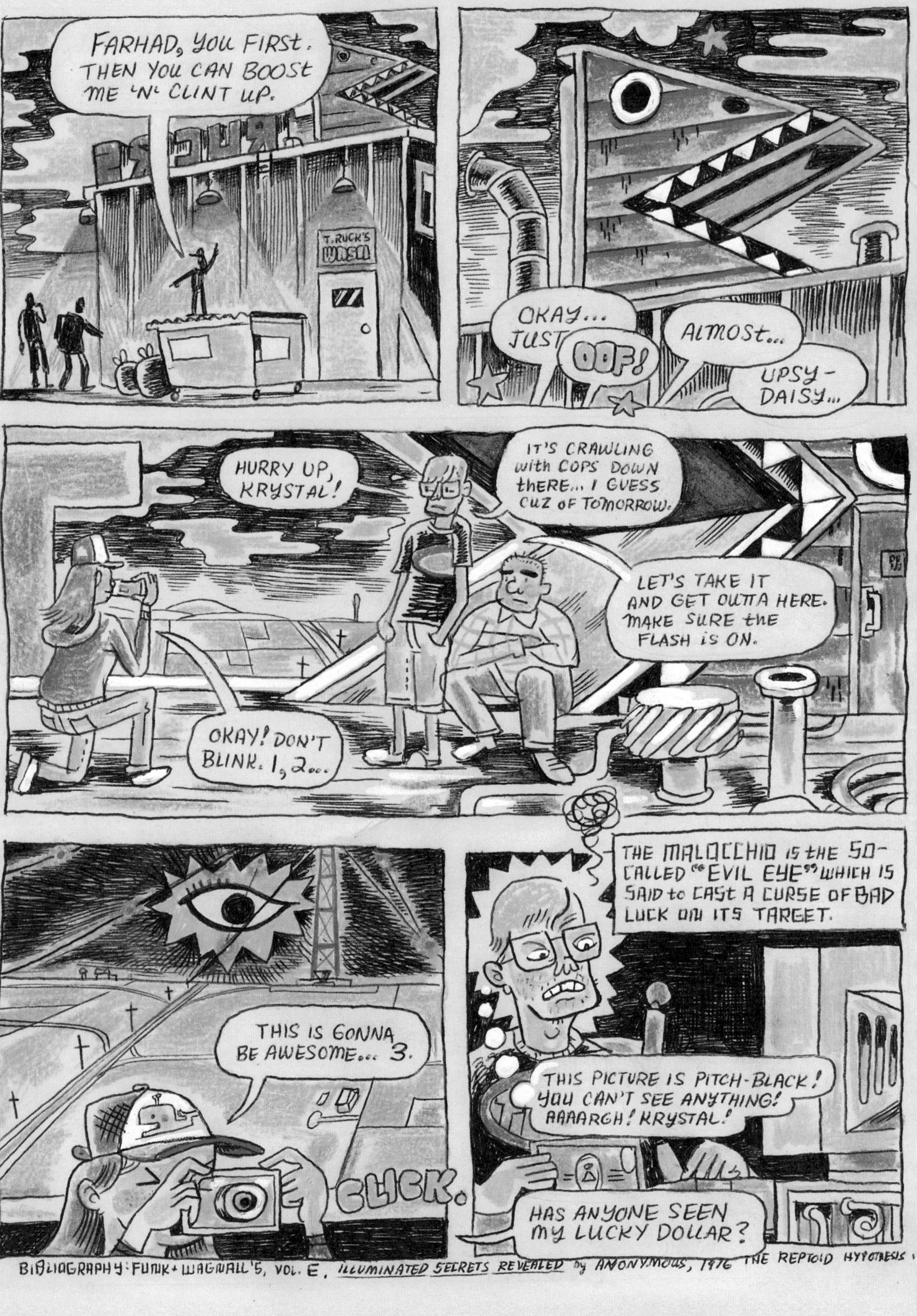
FARHAD, YOU FIRST. THEN YOU CAN BOOST ME 'N' CLINT UP.
T. RUCK'S WASH
OKAY... JUST
OOF!
ALMOST...
UPSY-DAISY...
HURRY UP, KRYSTAL!
IT'S CRAWLING WITH COPS DOWN THERE... I GUESS CUZ OF TOMORROW.
LET'S TAKE IT AND GET OUTTA HERE. MAKE SURE THE FLASH IS ON.
OKAY! DON'T BLINK. 1, 2...
THIS IS GONNA BE AWESOME... 3.
CLICK.
THE MALOCCHIO IS THE SO-CALLED "EVIL EYE" WHICH IS SAID TO CAST A CURSE OF BAD LUCK ON ITS TARGET.
THIS PICTURE IS PITCH-BLACK! YOU CAN'T SEE ANYTHING! AAAARGH! KRYSTAL!
HAS ANYONE SEEN MY LUCKY DOLLAR?

BIBLIOGRAPHY: FUNK + WAGNALL'S, VOL. E, ILLUMINATED SECRETS REVEALED by ANONYMOUS, 1976 THE REPTOID HYPOTHESIS.

MORNING ROUTINE

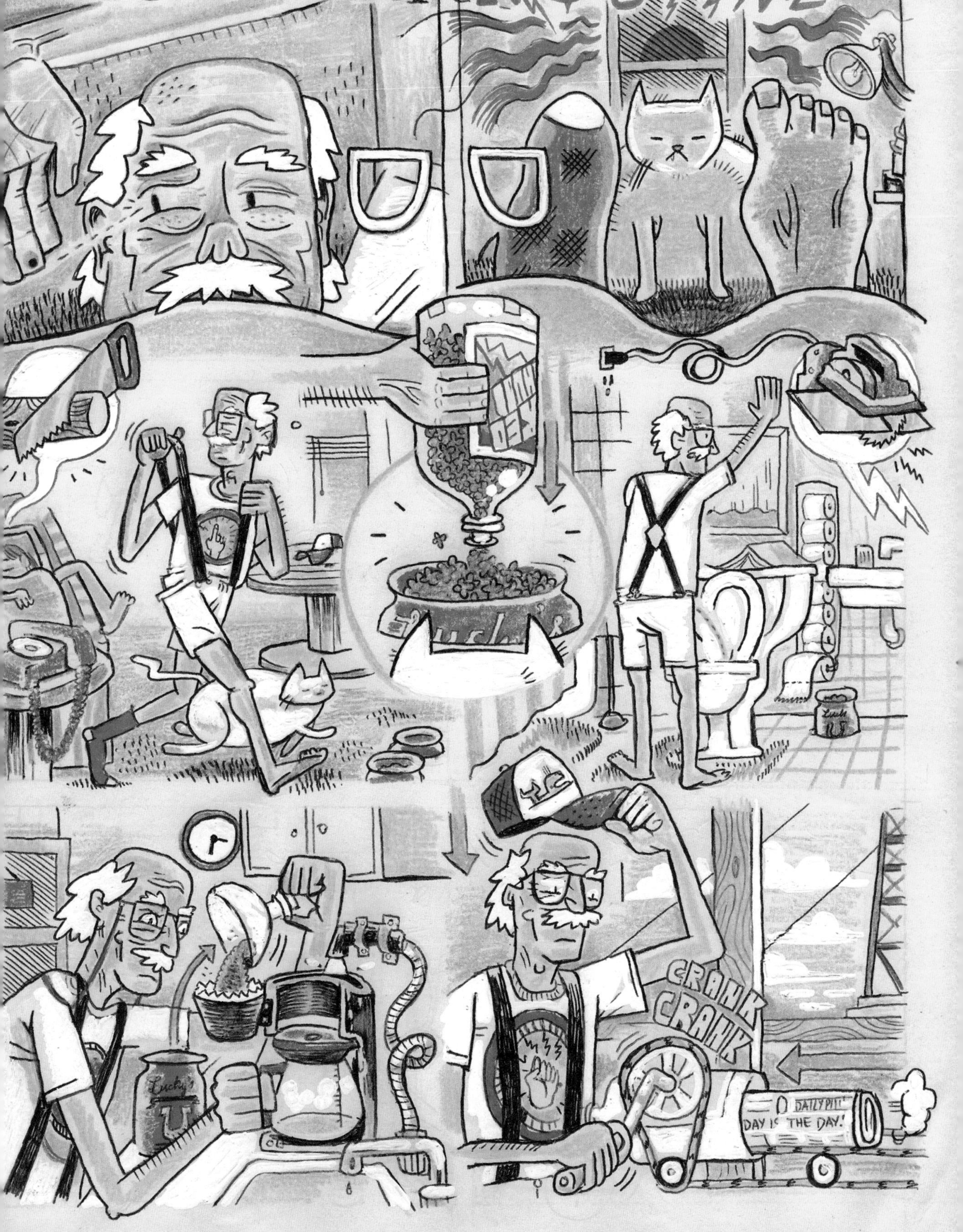
Lucky
Lucky's
CRANK
CRANK
DAILY PIT
DAY IS THE DAY!

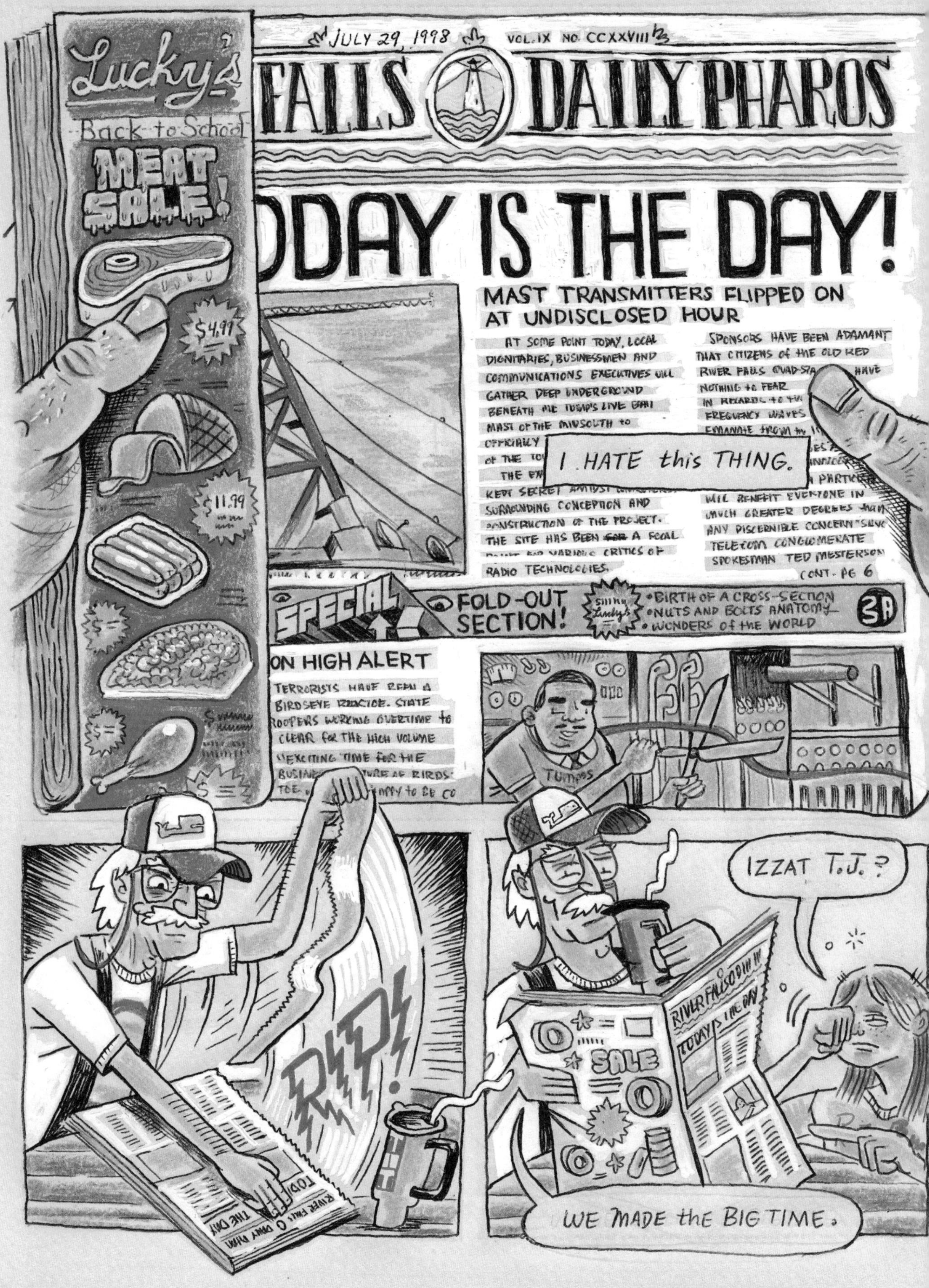
Lucky's
Back to School
MEAT SALE!
$4.99
$11.99
JULY 29, 1998
VOL. IX NO. CCXXVIII
FALLS DAILY PHAROS
ODAY IS THE DAY!
MAST TRANSMITTERS FLIPPED ON AT UNDISCLOSED HOUR
AT SOME POINT TODAY, LOCAL DIGNITARIES, BUSINESSMEN AND COMMUNICATIONS EXECUTIVES WILL GATHER DEEP UNDERGROUND
SURROUNDING CONCEPTION AND CONSTRUCTION OF THE PROJECT. THE SITE HAS BEEN A FOCAL
CRITICS OF RADIO TECHNOLOGIES.
SPONSORS HAVE BEEN ADAMANT THAT CITIZENS OF THE OLD RED RIVER FALLS
HAVE NOTHING TO FEAR
FREQUENCY WAVES
WILL BENEFIT EVERYONE IN MUCH GREATER DEGREES
ANY DISCERNIBLE CONCERN"
TELECOM CONGLOMERATE SPOKESMAN TED MESTERSON
CONT. PG 6
I HATE this THING.
SPECIAL
FOLD-OUT SECTION!
BIRTH OF A CROSS-SECTION
NUTS AND BOLTS ANATOMY
WONDERS OF THE WORLD
3A
ON HIGH ALERT
TERRORISTS
BIRDSEYE
STATE
OVERTIME TO CLEAR FOR THE HIGH VOLUME
EXCITING TIME FOR THE
RIP!
IZZAT T.J.?
SALE
TODAY IS THE DAY
WE MADE the BIG TIME.

BIRTH OF A CROSS-SECTION

Each of the 50 steel lattice sections that make up the vertical thrust of Tump's Live Bait™ Mast of the Midsouth are carefully constructed to interlock precisely, be strueturally indestructible, and withstand any weather condition. Here's how each section is created:

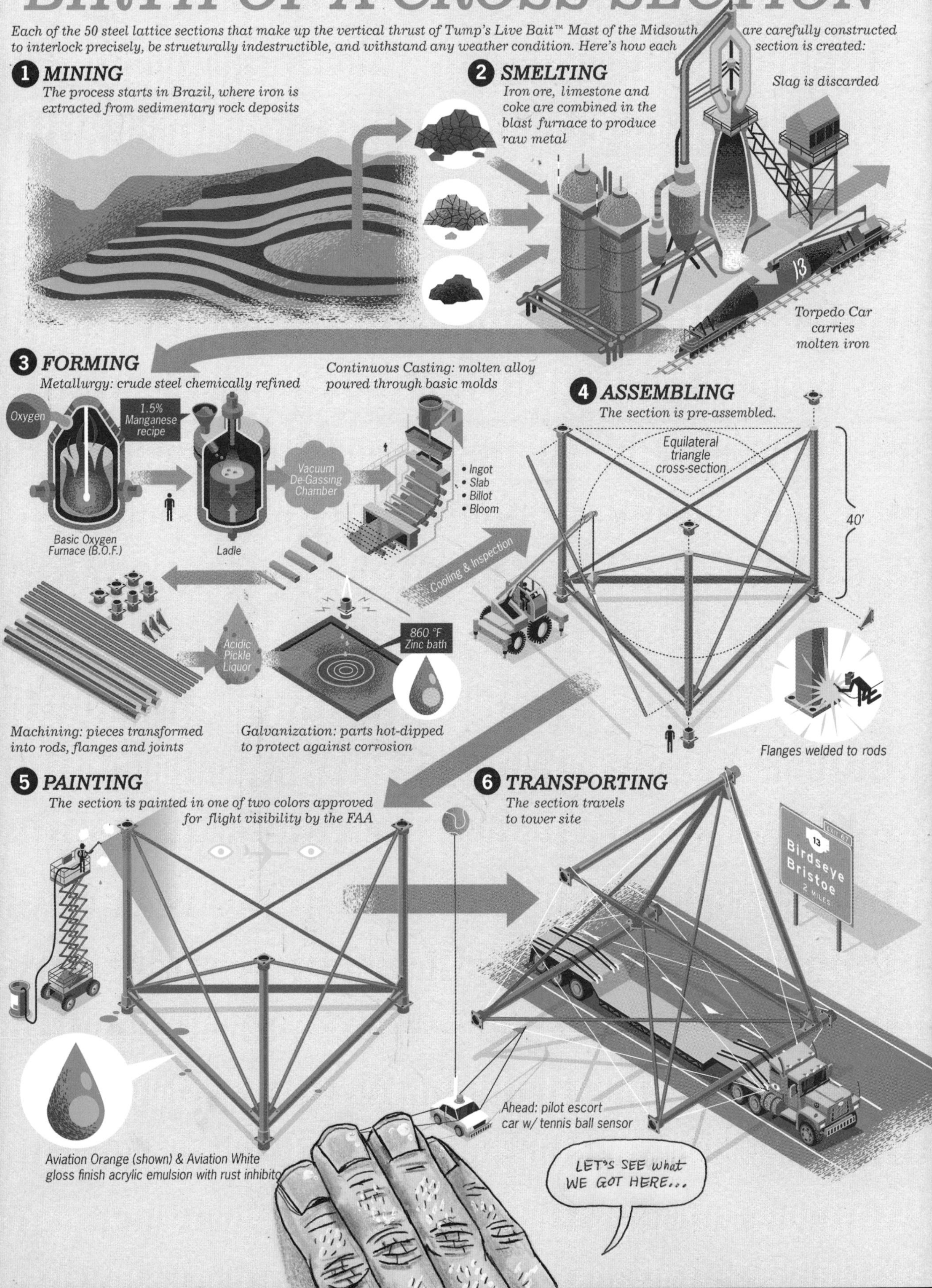

1 MINING
The process starts in Brazil, where iron is extracted from sedimentary rock deposits
2 SMELTING
Iron ore, limestone and coke are combined in the blast furnace to produce raw metal
Slag is discarded
13
Torpedo Car carries molten iron
3 FORMING
Metallurgy: crude steel chemically refined
Oxygen
1.5% Manganese recipe
Basic Oxygen Furnace (B.O.F.)
Ladle
Vacuum De-Gassing Chamber
Continuous Casting: molten alloy poured through basic molds
• Ingot
• Slab
• Billot
• Bloom
Cooling & Inspection
Acidic Pickle Liquor
860 °F Zinc bath
Machining: pieces transformed into rods, flanges and joints
Galvanization: parts hot-dipped to protect against corrosion
4 ASSEMBLING
The section is pre-assembled.
Equilateral triangle cross-section
40'
Flanges welded to rods
5 PAINTING
The section is painted in one of two colors approved for flight visibility by the FAA
Aviation Orange (shown) & Aviation White gloss finish acrylic emulsion with rust inhibito
6 TRANSPORTING
The section travels to tower site
EXIT 67
13
Birdseye
Bristoe
2 MILES
Ahead: pilot escort car w/ tennis ball sensor
LET'S SEE what WE GOT HERE...

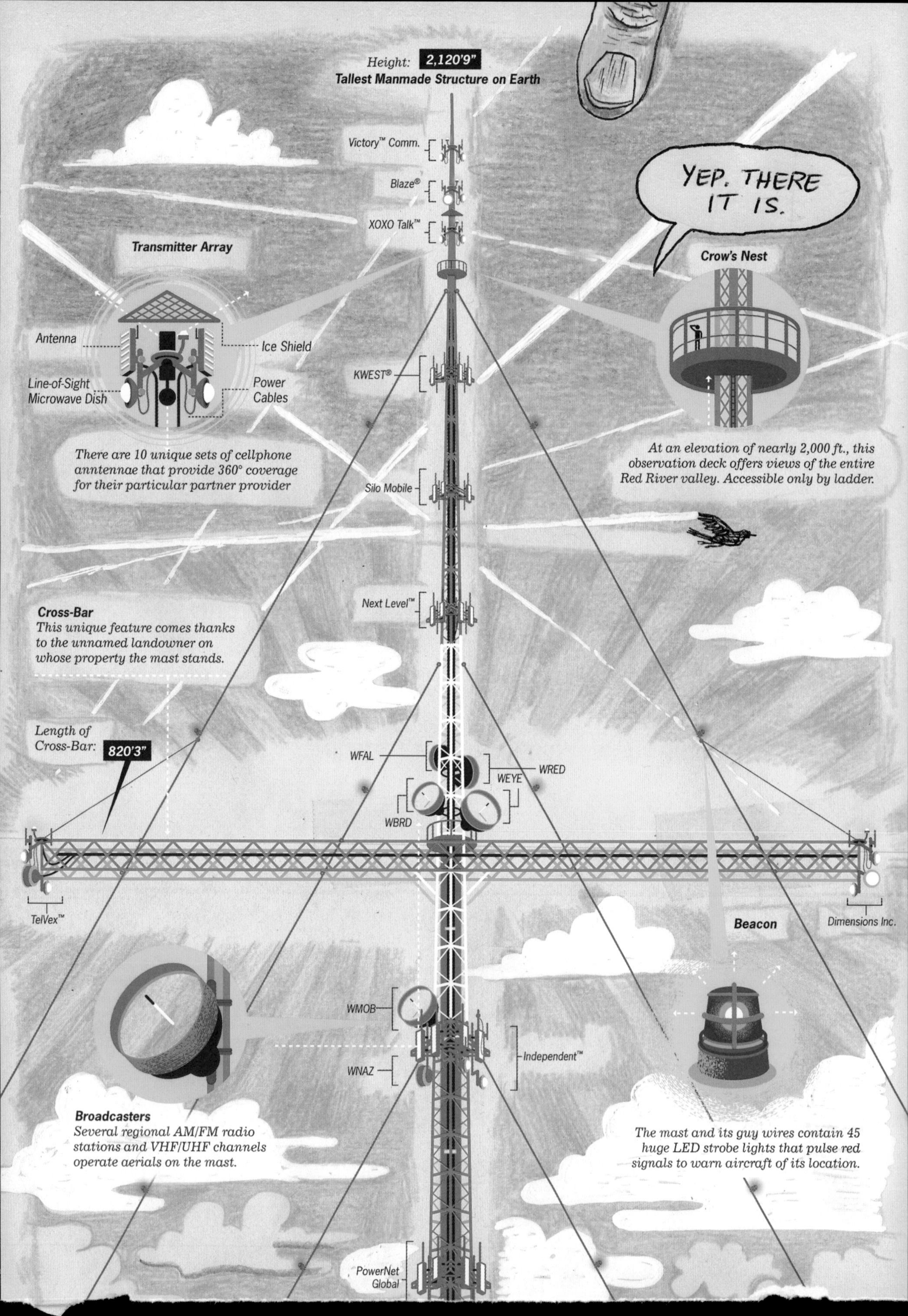

Height: 2,120'9"
Tallest Manmade Structure on Earth
Victory™ Comm.
Blaze®
XOXO Talk™
YEP. THERE IT IS.
Transmitter Array
Crow's Nest
Antenna
Ice Shield
Line-of-Sight Microwave Dish
Power Cables
KWEST®
There are 10 unique sets of cellphone anntennae that provide 360° coverage for their particular partner provider
At an elevation of nearly 2,000 ft., this observation deck offers views of the entire Red River valley. Accessible only by ladder.
Silo Mobile
Next Level™
Cross-Bar
This unique feature comes thanks to the unnamed landowner on whose property the mast stands.
Length of Cross-Bar: 820'3"
WFAL
WRED
WEYE
WBRD
TelVex™
Dimensions Inc.
Beacon
WMOB
Independent™
WNAZ
Broadcasters
Several regional AM/FM radio stations and VHF/UHF channels operate aerials on the mast.
The mast and its guy wires contain 45 huge LED strobe lights that pulse red signals to warn aircraft of its location.
PowerNet Global

WONDERS of the WORLD

Although ineligible for title of "World's Tallest Building" (because of no habitable living space) or "World's Tallest Freestanding Tower" (because of the presence of guy wires), Tump's Live Bait™ Mast of the Midsouth is officially the tallest* man-made structure on earth, at least until rumored top-secret skyscrapers under construction in the Middle East are completed next year.

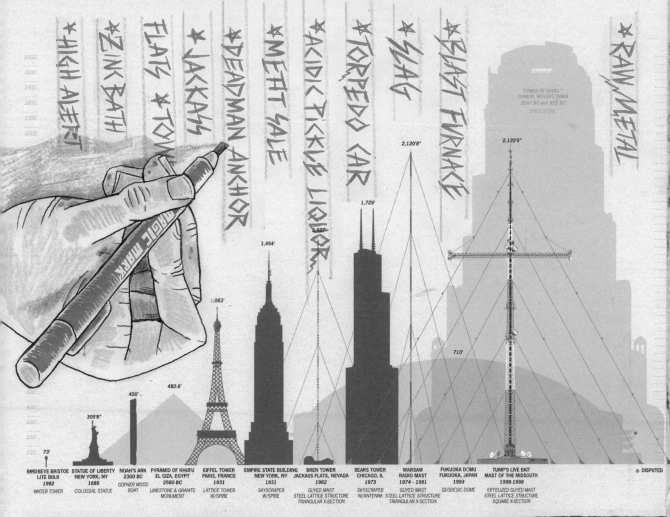

★HIGH ALERT ★ZINK BATH ★FLATS ★TOW ★JACKASS ★DEADMAN ANCHOR ★MEAT SALE ★ACIDIC TICKLE LIQUOR ★TORPEDO CAR ★SLAG ★BLAST FURNACE ★RAW METAL

TOWER OF BABEL*
SHINAR, MESOPOTAMIA
2247 BC and 952 BC
BRICK/STONE

2,120'8"
2,120'9"

1,729'
710'
1,527'
1,454'
1,063'
480.6'
450'
305'6"
73'

BIRDSEYE BRISTOE LITE BULB	STATUE OF LIBERTY NEW YORK, NY	NOAH'S ARK	PYRAMID OF KHUFU EL GIZA, EGYPT	EIFFEL TOWER PARIS, FRANCE	EMPIRE STATE BUILDING NEW YORK, NY	BREN TOWER JACKASS FLATS, NEVADA	SEARS TOWER CHICAGO, IL	WARSAW RADIO MAST	FUKUOKA DOMU FUKUOKA, JAPAN	TUMP'S LIVE BAIT MAST OF THE MIDSOUTH
1982	1886	2300 BC	2560 BC	1931	1931	1962	1973	1974 - 1991	1993	1998-1998
WATER TOWER	COLOSSAL STATUE	GOPHER WOOD BOAT	LIMESTONE & GRANITE MONUMENT	LATTICE TOWER W/SPIRE	SKYSCRAPER W/SPIRE	GUYED MAST STEEL LATTICE STRUCTURE TRIANGULAR X-SECTION	SKYSCRAPER W/ANTENNA	GUYED MAST STEEL LATTICE STRUCTURE TRIANGULAR X-SECTION	GEODESIC DOME	EFFELIZED GUYED MAST STEEL LATTICE STRUCTURE SQUARE X-SECTION

* DISPUTED

THERE'S LIKE A ZILLION GOOD BAND NAMES in HERE.

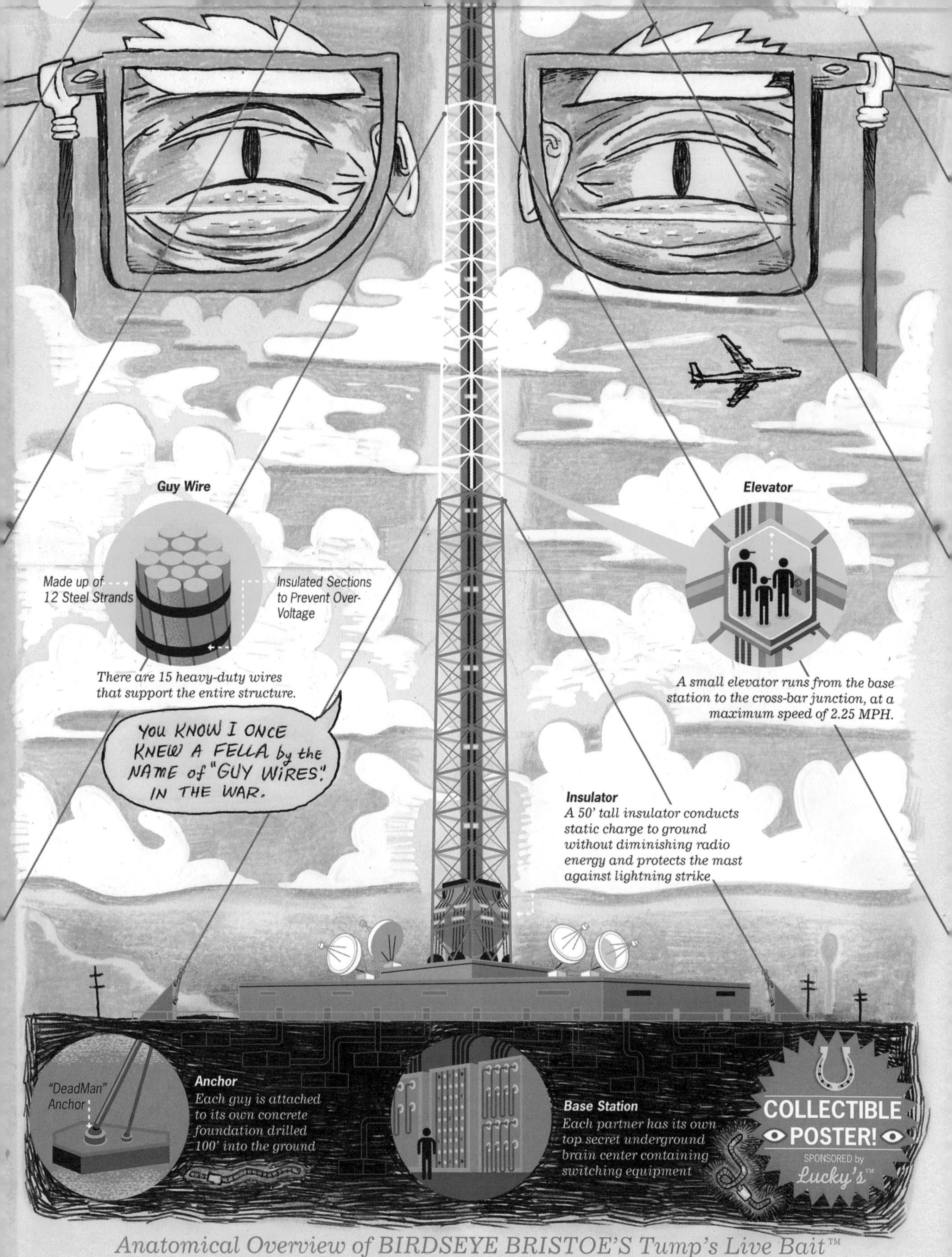
Guy Wire
Made up of 12 Steel Strands
Insulated Sections to Prevent Over-Voltage
There are 15 heavy-duty wires that support the entire structure.
YOU KNOW I ONCE KNEW A FELLA by the NAME of "GUY WIRES" IN THE WAR.
Elevator
A small elevator runs from the base station to the cross-bar junction, at a maximum speed of 2.25 MPH.
Insulator
A 50' tall insulator conducts static charge to ground without diminishing radio energy and protects the mast against lightning strike
"DeadMan" Anchor
Anchor
Each guy is attached to its own concrete foundation drilled 100' into the ground
Base Station
Each partner has its own top secret underground brain center containing switching equipment
COLLECTIBLE POSTER!
SPONSORED by Lucky's™

Anatomical Overview of BIRDSEYE BRISTOE'S Tump's Live Bait™

MAST of the MID-SOUTH!

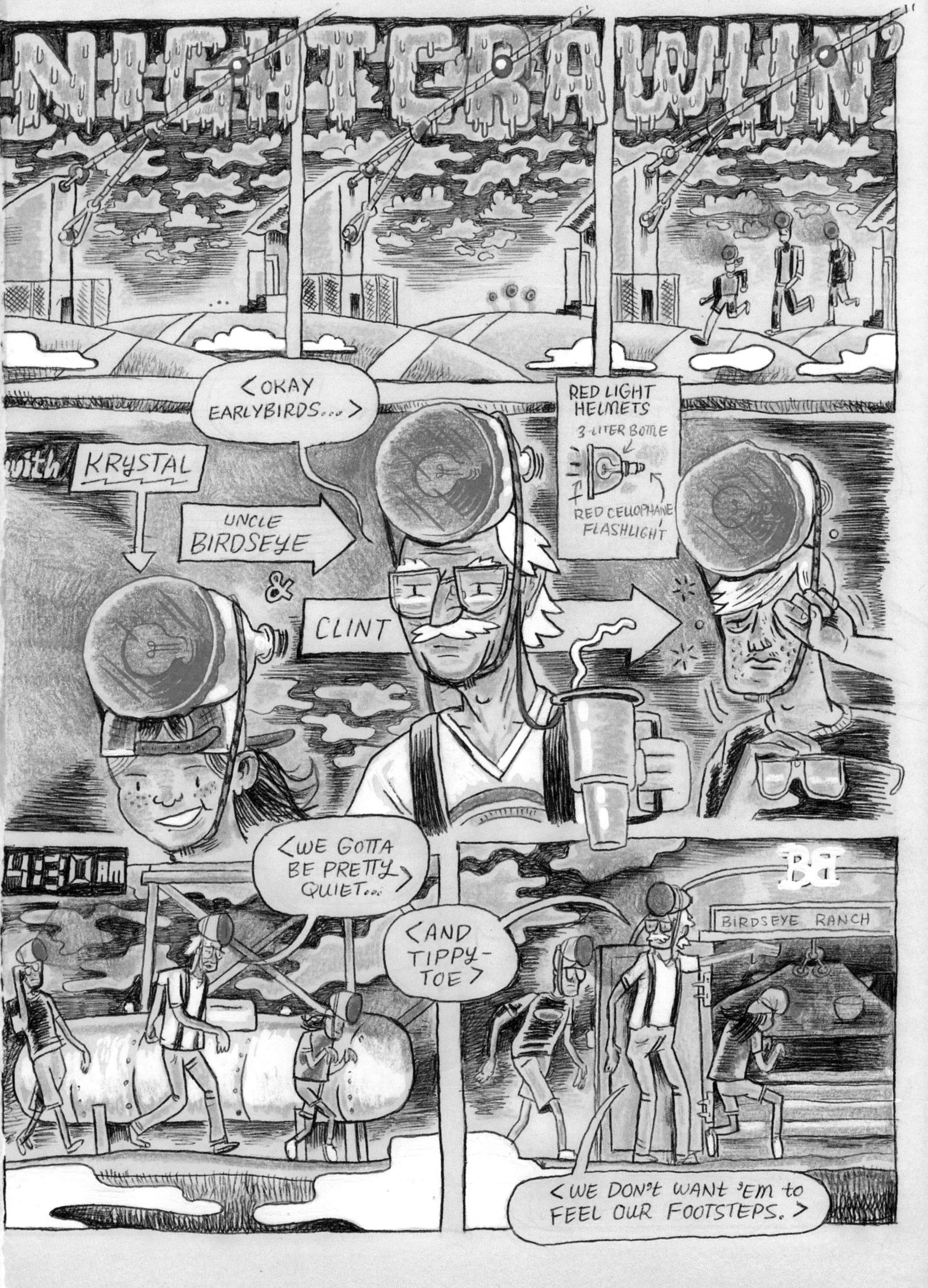
NIGHTCRAWLIN'
<OKAY EARLYBIRDS...>
with KRYSTAL
UNCLE BIRDSEYE
&
CLINT
RED LIGHT HELMETS
3-LITER BOTTLE
RED CELLOPHANE
FLASHLIGHT
4:30 AM
<WE GOTTA BE PRETTY QUIET...>
<AND TIPPY-TOE>
BIRDSEYE RANCH
<WE DON'T WANT 'EM TO FEEL OUR FOOTSTEPS.>

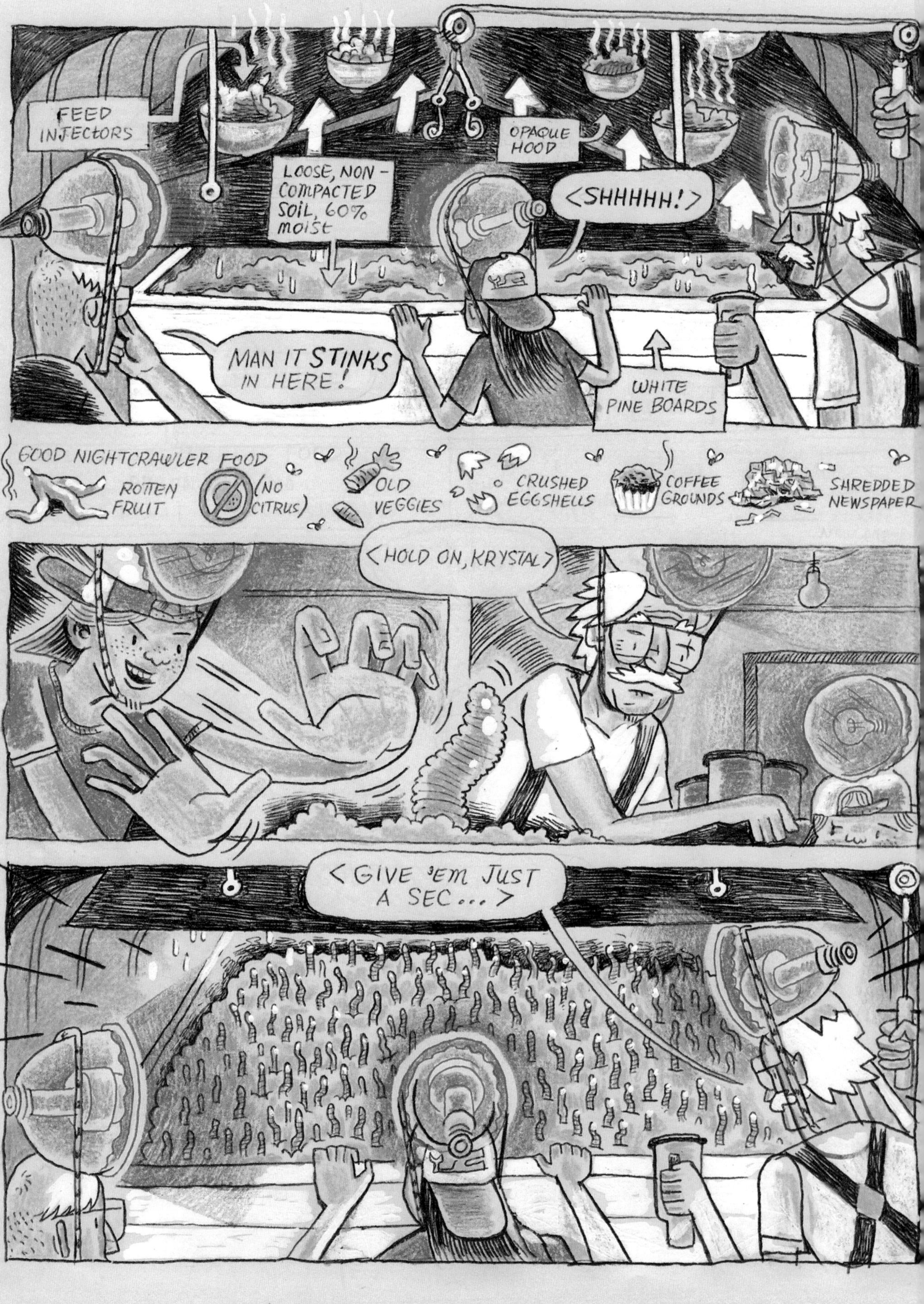
FEED INJECTORS
LOOSE, NON-COMPACTED SOIL, 60% moist
OPAQUE HOOD
<SHHHHH!>
MAN IT STINKS IN HERE!
WHITE PINE BOARDS
GOOD NIGHTCRAWLER FOOD
ROTTEN FRUIT
(NO CITRUS)
OLD VEGGIES
CRUSHED EGGSHELLS
COFFEE GROUNDS
SHREDDED NEWSPAPER
<HOLD ON, KRYSTAL>
<GIVE 'EM JUST A SEC...>

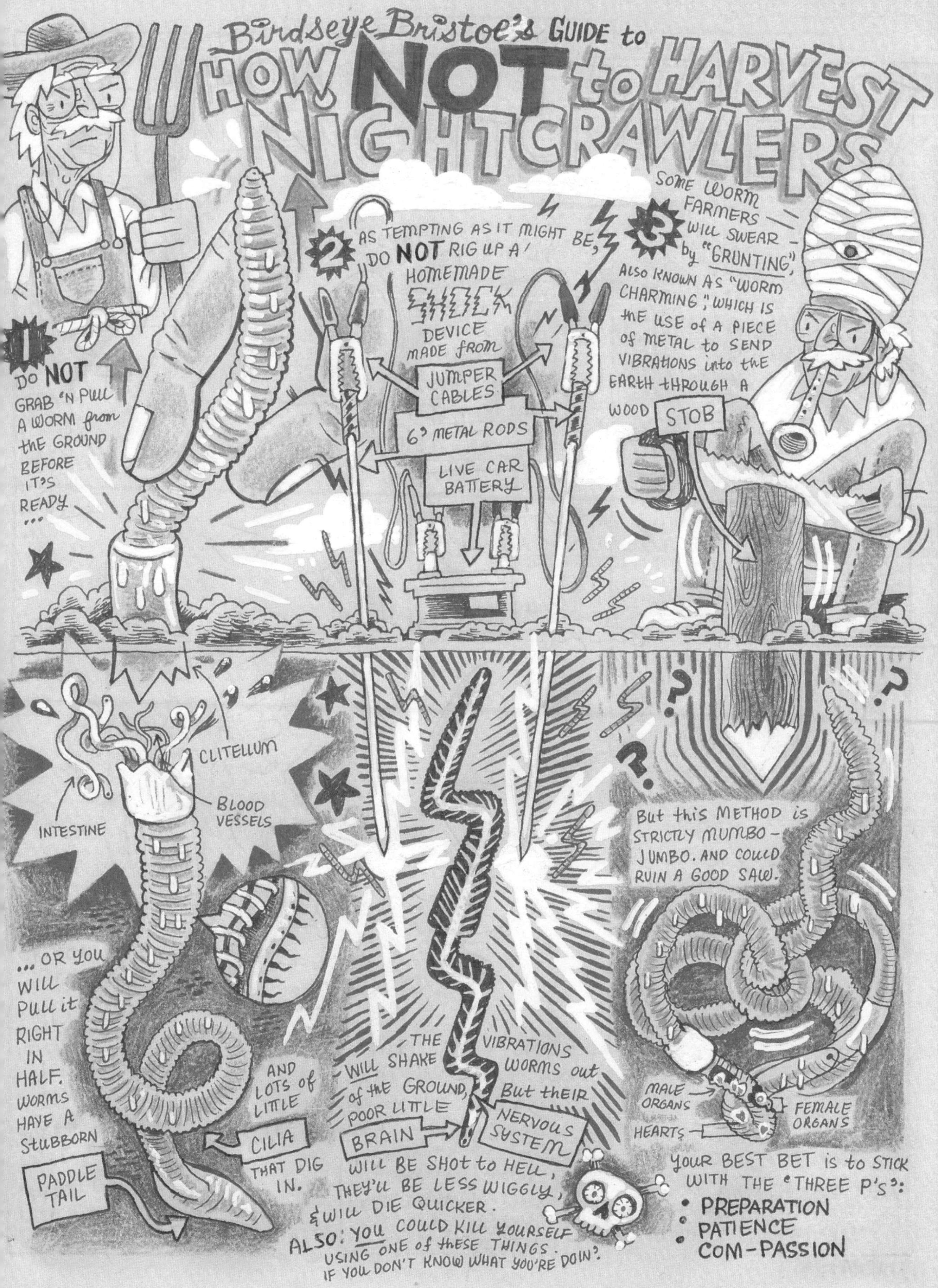

Birdseye Bristol's GUIDE to
HOW NOT to HARVEST NIGHTCRAWLERS
1 DO NOT GRAB 'N PULL A WORM from the GROUND BEFORE IT'S READY...
...OR YOU WILL PULL it RIGHT IN HALF. WORMS HAVE A STUBBORN
PADDLE TAIL
AND LOTS of LITTLE
CILIA
THAT DIG IN.
CLITELLUM
INTESTINE
BLOOD VESSELS
2 AS TEMPTING AS IT MIGHT BE, DO NOT RIG UP A HOMEMADE SHOCK DEVICE made from
JUMPER CABLES
6' METAL RODS
LIVE CAR BATTERY
THE VIBRATIONS WILL SHAKE WORMS out of the GROUND, But their POOR LITTLE
BRAIN
NERVOUS SYSTEM
WILL BE SHOT to HELL, THEY'LL BE LESS WIGGLY, & WILL DIE QUICKER.
ALSO: YOU COULD KILL YOURSELF USING ONE of these THINGS. IF YOU DON'T KNOW WHAT YOU'RE DOIN'.
3 SOME WORM FARMERS WILL SWEAR by "GRUNTING", ALSO KNOWN AS "WORM CHARMING," WHICH IS the USE of A PIECE of METAL to SEND VIBRATIONS into the EARTH through A WOOD
STOB
But this METHOD is STRICTLY MUMBO-JUMBO. AND COULD RUIN A GOOD SAW.
MALE ORGANS
FEMALE ORGANS
HEARTS
YOUR BEST BET is to STICK WITH THE "THREE P's":
PREPARATION
PATIENCE
COM-PASSION

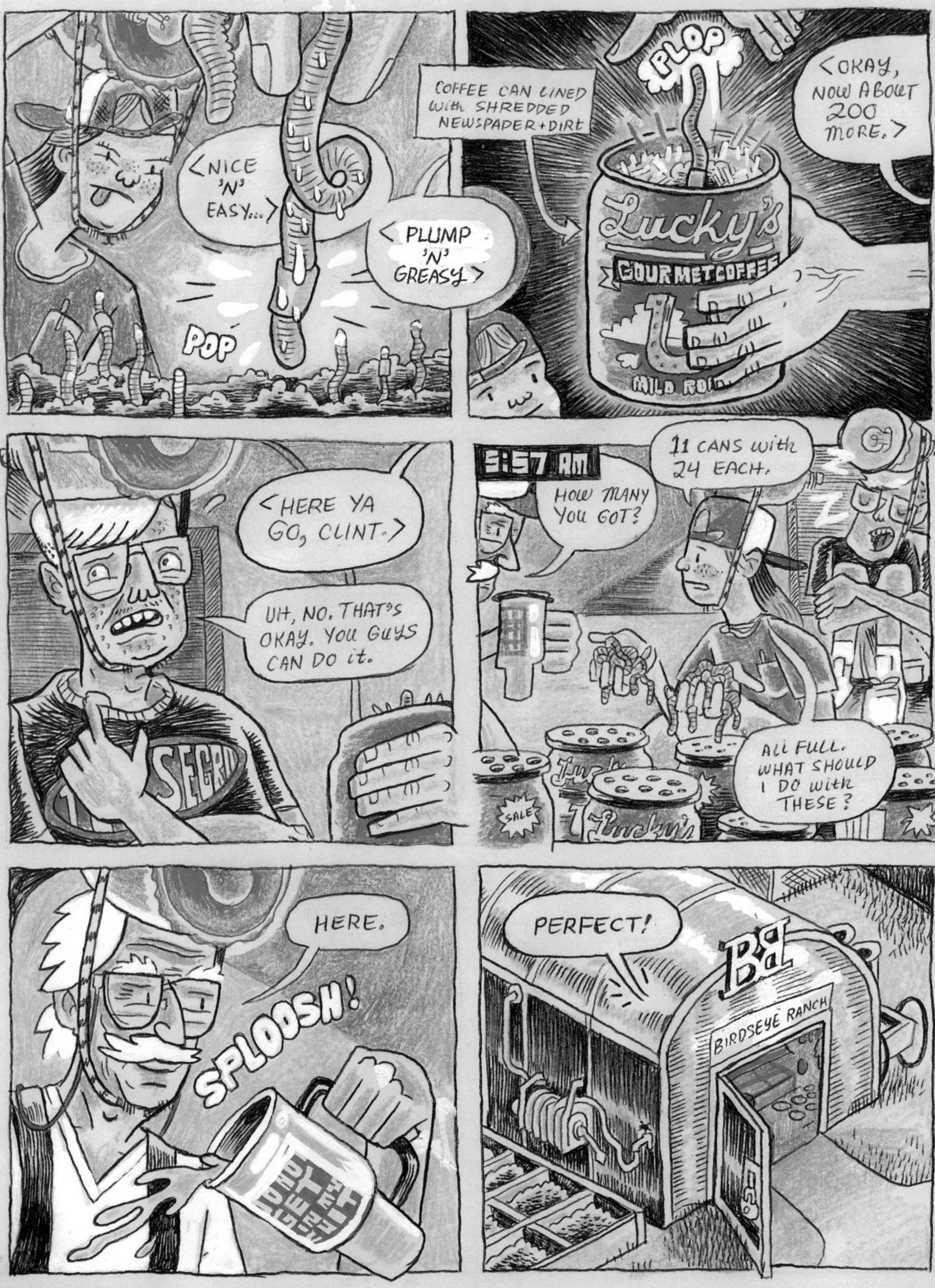

<NICE 'N' EASY...>
<PLUMP 'N' GREASY>
POP
COFFEE CAN LINED WITH SHREDDED NEWSPAPER + DIRT
PLOP
<OKAY, NOW ABOUT 200 MORE.>
Lucky's
GOURMET COFFEE
MILD RO
<HERE YA GO, CLINT.>
UH, NO. THAT'S OKAY. YOU GUYS CAN DO IT.
5:57 AM
HOW MANY YOU GOT?
11 CANS WITH 24 EACH.
ALL FULL. WHAT SHOULD I DO WITH THESE?
HERE.
SPLOOSH!
PERFECT!
BIRDSEYE RANCH

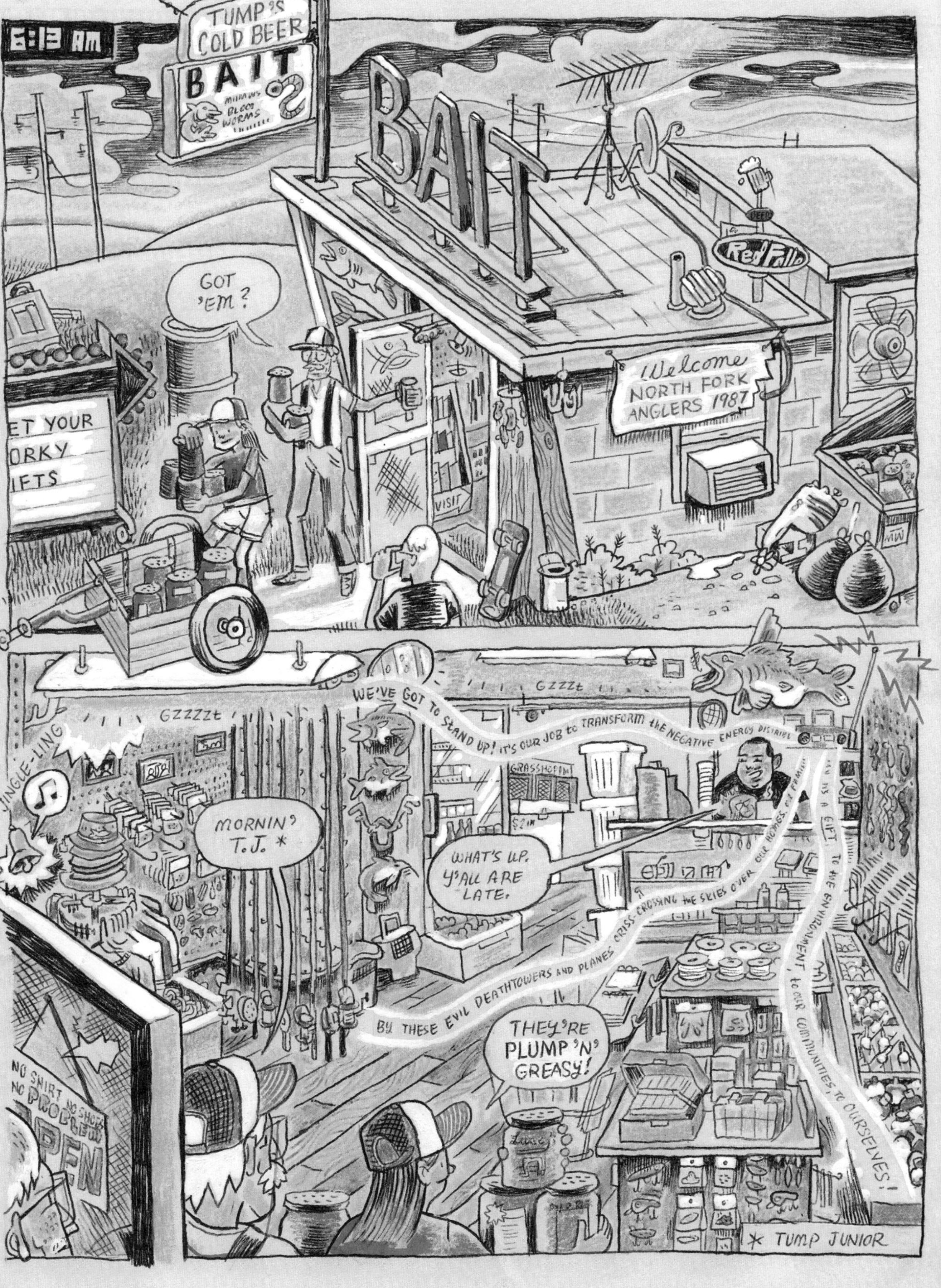

6:13 AM
TUMP'S COLD BEER
BAIT
MINNOWS BLOOD WORMS
BAIT
Red Fallo
WELCOME NORTH FORK ANGLERS 1987
GOT 'EM?
ET YOUR
ORKY
IFTS
VISIT
GZZZZt
GZZZt
JINGLE-LING
MORNIN' T.J. *
GRASSHOPPERS
WHAT'S UP. Y'ALL ARE LATE.
WE'VE GOT TO STAND UP! IT'S OUR JOB TO TRANSFORM THE NEGATIVE ENERGY DISTRIB
BY THESE EVIL DEATHTOWERS AND PLANES CRISS-CROSSING THE SKIES OVER OUR HOMES, OUR FAMI
AND IT'S A GIFT, TO THE ENVIRONMENT, TO OUR COMMUNITIES, TO OURSELVES!
THEY'RE PLUMP 'N' GREASY!
NO SHIRT NO SHOES NO PROBLEM
OPEN
* TUMP JUNIOR

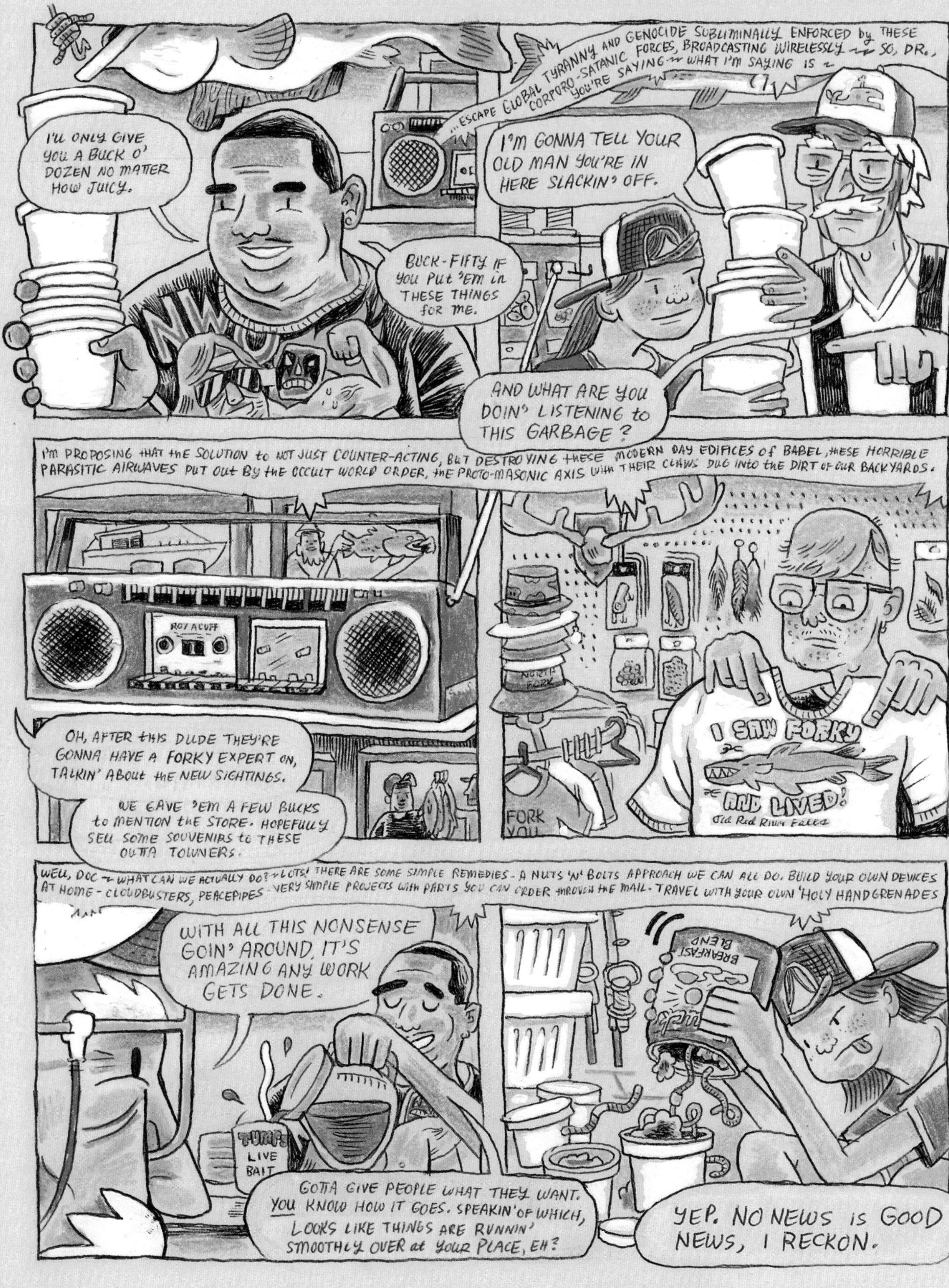

...ESCAPE GLOBAL TYRANNY AND GENOCIDE SUBLIMINALLY ENFORCED BY THESE CORPORO-SATANIC FORCES, BROADCASTING WIRELESSLY — SO, DR., YOU'RE SAYING — WHAT I'M SAYING IS —
I'LL ONLY GIVE YOU A BUCK O' DOZEN NO MATTER HOW JUICY.
BUCK-FIFTY IF YOU PUT 'EM IN THESE THINGS FOR ME.
I'M GONNA TELL YOUR OLD MAN YOU'RE IN HERE SLACKIN' OFF.
AND WHAT ARE YOU DOIN' LISTENING TO THIS GARBAGE?
I'M PROPOSING THAT THE SOLUTION TO NOT JUST COUNTER-ACTING, BUT DESTROYING THESE MODERN DAY EDIFICES OF BABEL, THESE HORRIBLE PARASITIC AIRWAVES PUT OUT BY THE OCCULT WORLD ORDER, THE PROTO-MASONIC AXIS WITH THEIR CLAWS DUG INTO THE DIRT OF OUR BACKYARDS.
ROY ACUFF
OH, AFTER THIS DUDE THEY'RE GONNA HAVE A FORKY EXPERT ON, TALKIN' ABOUT THE NEW SIGHTINGS.
WE GAVE 'EM A FEW BUCKS TO MENTION THE STORE. HOPEFULLY SELL SOME SOUVENIRS TO THESE OUTTA TOWNERS.
NORTH FORK
FORK YOU
I SAW FORKY AND LIVED!
Old Red River Falls
WELL, DOC — WHAT CAN WE ACTUALLY DO? — LOTS! THERE ARE SOME SIMPLE REMEDIES - A NUTS 'N' BOLTS APPROACH WE CAN ALL DO. BUILD YOUR OWN DEVICES AT HOME - CLOUDBUSTERS, PEACEPIPES - VERY SIMPLE PROJECTS WITH PARTS YOU CAN ORDER THROUGH THE MAIL. TRAVEL WITH YOUR OWN 'HOLY HANDGRENADES
WITH ALL THIS NONSENSE GOIN' AROUND, IT'S AMAZING ANY WORK GETS DONE.
BREAKFAST BLEND
TUMP'S LIVE BAIT
GOTTA GIVE PEOPLE WHAT THEY WANT. YOU KNOW HOW IT GOES. SPEAKIN' OF WHICH, LOOKS LIKE THINGS ARE RUNNIN' SMOOTHLY OVER AT YOUR PLACE, EH?
YEP. NO NEWS IS GOOD NEWS, I RECKON.

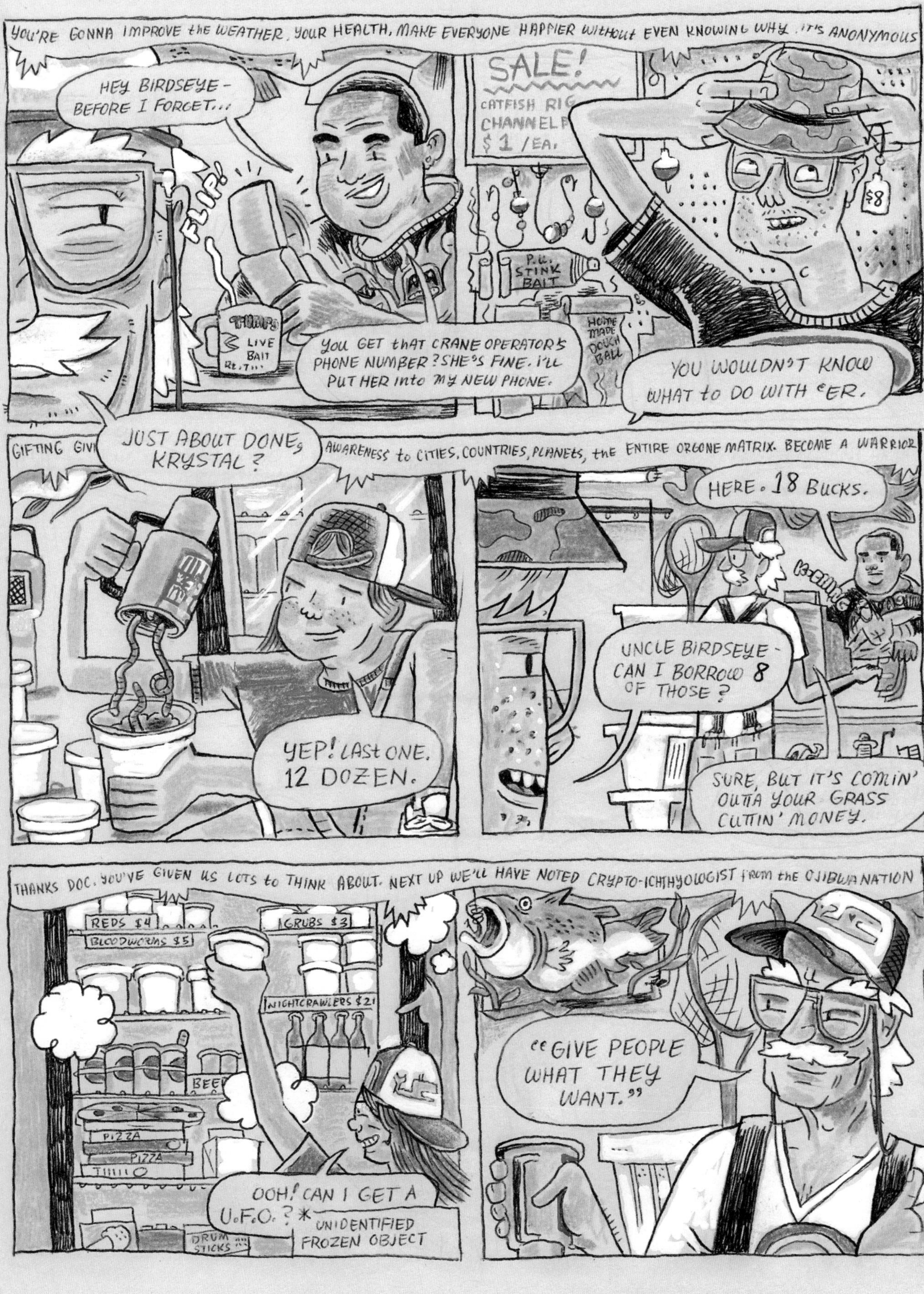
YOU'RE GONNA IMPROVE THE WEATHER, YOUR HEALTH, MAKE EVERYONE HAPPIER WITHOUT EVEN KNOWING WHY. IT'S ANONYMOUS
HEY BIRDSEYE - BEFORE I FORGET...
FLIP!
SALE! CATFISH RIG CHANNEL $1/EA.
$8
P.U. STINK BAIT
TIMPS LIVE BAIT
HOME MADE DOUGH BALL
YOU GET THAT CRANE OPERATOR'S PHONE NUMBER? SHE'S FINE. I'LL PUT HER INTO MY NEW PHONE.
YOU WOULDN'T KNOW WHAT TO DO WITH 'ER.
GIFTING GIV
AWARENESS TO CITIES, COUNTRIES, PLANETS, THE ENTIRE ORGONE MATRIX. BECOME A WARRIOR
JUST ABOUT DONE, KRYSTAL?
YEP! LAST ONE. 12 DOZEN.
HERE. 18 BUCKS.
UNCLE BIRDSEYE - CAN I BORROW 8 OF THOSE?
SURE, BUT IT'S COMIN' OUTTA YOUR GRASS CUTTIN' MONEY.
THANKS DOC. YOU'VE GIVEN US LOTS TO THINK ABOUT. NEXT UP WE'LL HAVE NOTED CRYPTO-ICHTHYOLOGIST FROM THE OJIBWA NATION
REDS $4
GRUBS $3
BLOODWORMS $5
NIGHTCRAWLERS $2
BEER
PIZZA
PIZZA
DRUM STICKS
OOH! CAN I GET A U.F.O.?*
*UNIDENTIFIED FROZEN OBJECT
"GIVE PEOPLE WHAT THEY WANT."

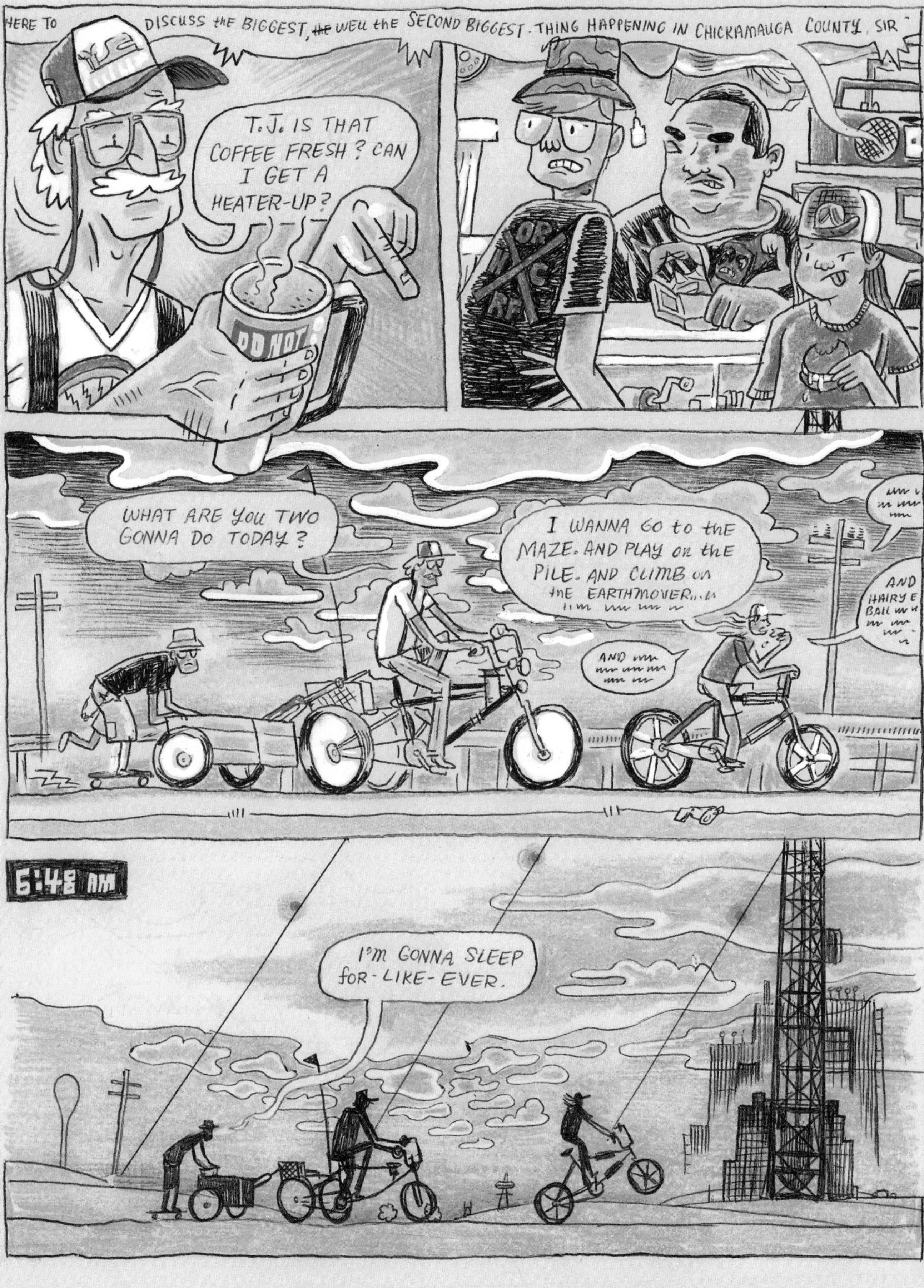

HERE TO DISCUSS the BIGGEST, the well the SECOND BIGGEST - THING HAPPENING IN CHICKAMAUGA COUNTY, SIR -
T.J. IS THAT COFFEE FRESH? CAN I GET A HEATER-UP?
DO NOT
WHAT ARE YOU TWO GONNA DO TODAY?
I WANNA GO to the MAZE. AND PLAY on the PILE. AND CLIMB on the EARTHMOVER...
AND
AND HAIRY BALL
6:48 AM
I'M GONNA SLEEP for-LIKE-EVER.

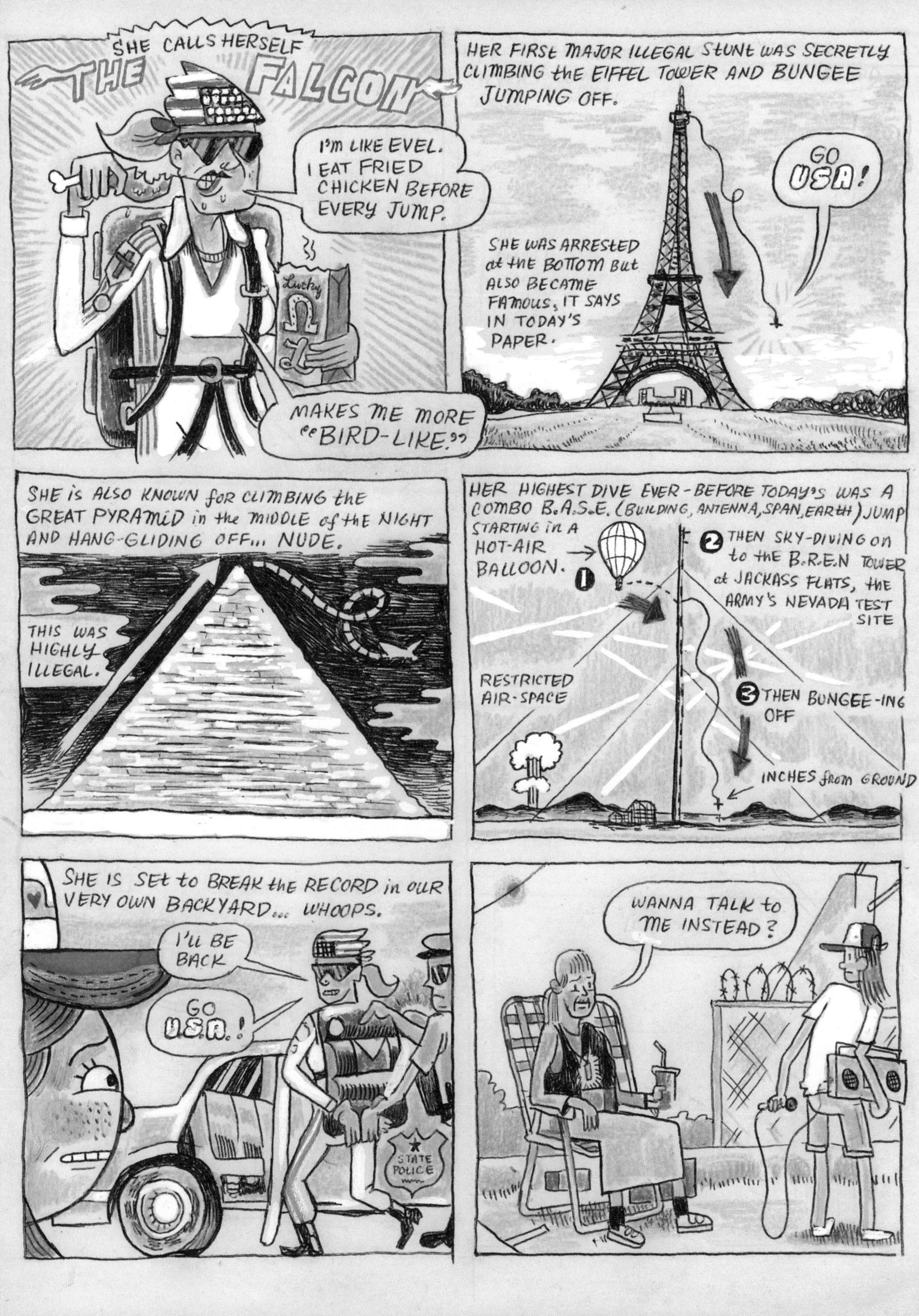
SHE CALLS HERSELF
THE FALCON
I'M LIKE EVEL. I EAT FRIED CHICKEN BEFORE EVERY JUMP.
Lucky
MAKES ME MORE "BIRD-LIKE."
HER FIRST MAJOR ILLEGAL STUNT WAS SECRETLY CLIMBING THE EIFFEL TOWER AND BUNGEE JUMPING OFF.
GO USA!
SHE WAS ARRESTED AT THE BOTTOM BUT ALSO BECAME FAMOUS, IT SAYS IN TODAY'S PAPER.
SHE IS ALSO KNOWN FOR CLIMBING THE GREAT PYRAMID IN THE MIDDLE OF THE NIGHT AND HANG-GLIDING OFF... NUDE.
THIS WAS HIGHLY ILLEGAL.
HER HIGHEST DIVE EVER - BEFORE TODAY'S WAS A COMBO B.A.S.E. (BUILDING, ANTENNA, SPAN, EARTH) JUMP
STARTING IN A HOT-AIR BALLOON.
1
2 THEN SKY-DIVING ON TO THE B.R.E.N TOWER AT JACKASS FLATS, THE ARMY'S NEVADA TEST SITE
RESTRICTED AIR-SPACE
3 THEN BUNGEE-ING OFF
INCHES FROM GROUND
SHE IS SET TO BREAK THE RECORD IN OUR VERY OWN BACKYARD... WHOOPS.
I'LL BE BACK
GO U.S.A.!
STATE POLICE
WANNA TALK TO ME INSTEAD?

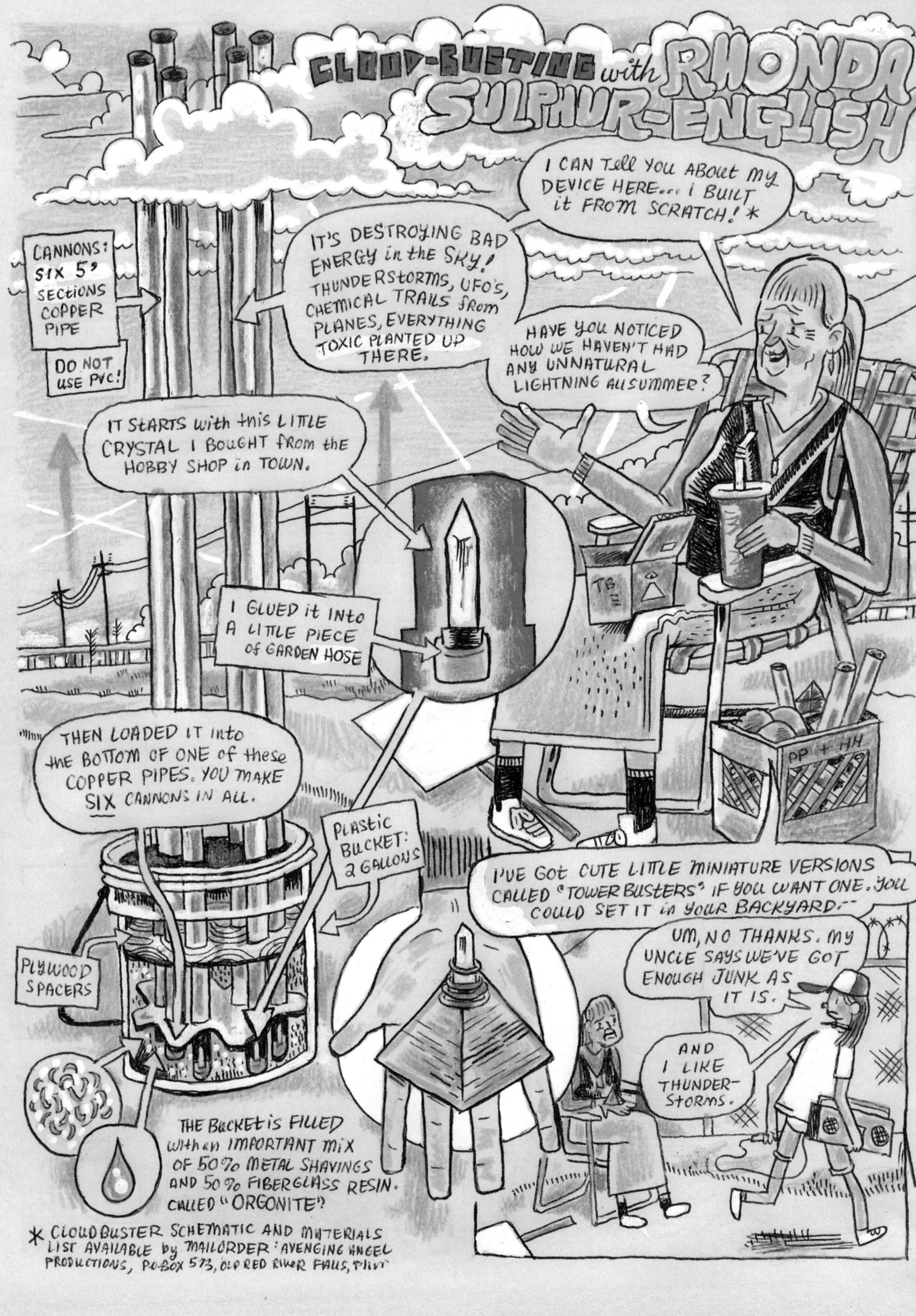
CLOUD-BUSTING with RHONDA SULPHUR-ENGLISH
I CAN TELL YOU ABOUT MY DEVICE HERE... I BUILT IT FROM SCRATCH! *
IT'S DESTROYING BAD ENERGY in the SKY! THUNDERSTORMS, UFO'S, CHEMICAL TRAILS from PLANES, EVERYTHING TOXIC PLANTED UP THERE.
CANNONS: SIX 5' SECTIONS COPPER PIPE
DO NOT USE PVC!
HAVE YOU NOTICED HOW WE HAVEN'T HAD ANY UNNATURAL LIGHTNING ALL SUMMER?
IT STARTS with this LITTLE CRYSTAL I BOUGHT from the HOBBY SHOP in TOWN.
I GLUED it INTO A LITTLE PIECE of GARDEN HOSE
TB
PP + HH
THEN LOADED IT into the BOTTOM OF ONE of these COPPER PIPES. YOU MAKE SIX CANNONS IN ALL.
PLASTIC BUCKET: 2 GALLONS
PLYWOOD SPACERS
THE BUCKET IS FILLED WITH AN IMPORTANT MIX OF 50% METAL SHAVINGS AND 50% FIBERGLASS RESIN. CALLED "ORGONITE"
I'VE GOT CUTE LITTLE MINIATURE VERSIONS CALLED "TOWER BUSTERS" IF YOU WANT ONE. YOU COULD SET IT IN YOUR BACKYARD.
UM, NO THANKS. MY UNCLE SAYS WE'VE GOT ENOUGH JUNK AS IT IS.
AND I LIKE THUNDER-STORMS.
* CLOUDBUSTER SCHEMATIC AND MATERIALS LIST AVAILABLE by MAILORDER: AVENGING ANGEL PRODUCTIONS, P.O. BOX 573, OLD RED RIVER FALLS,

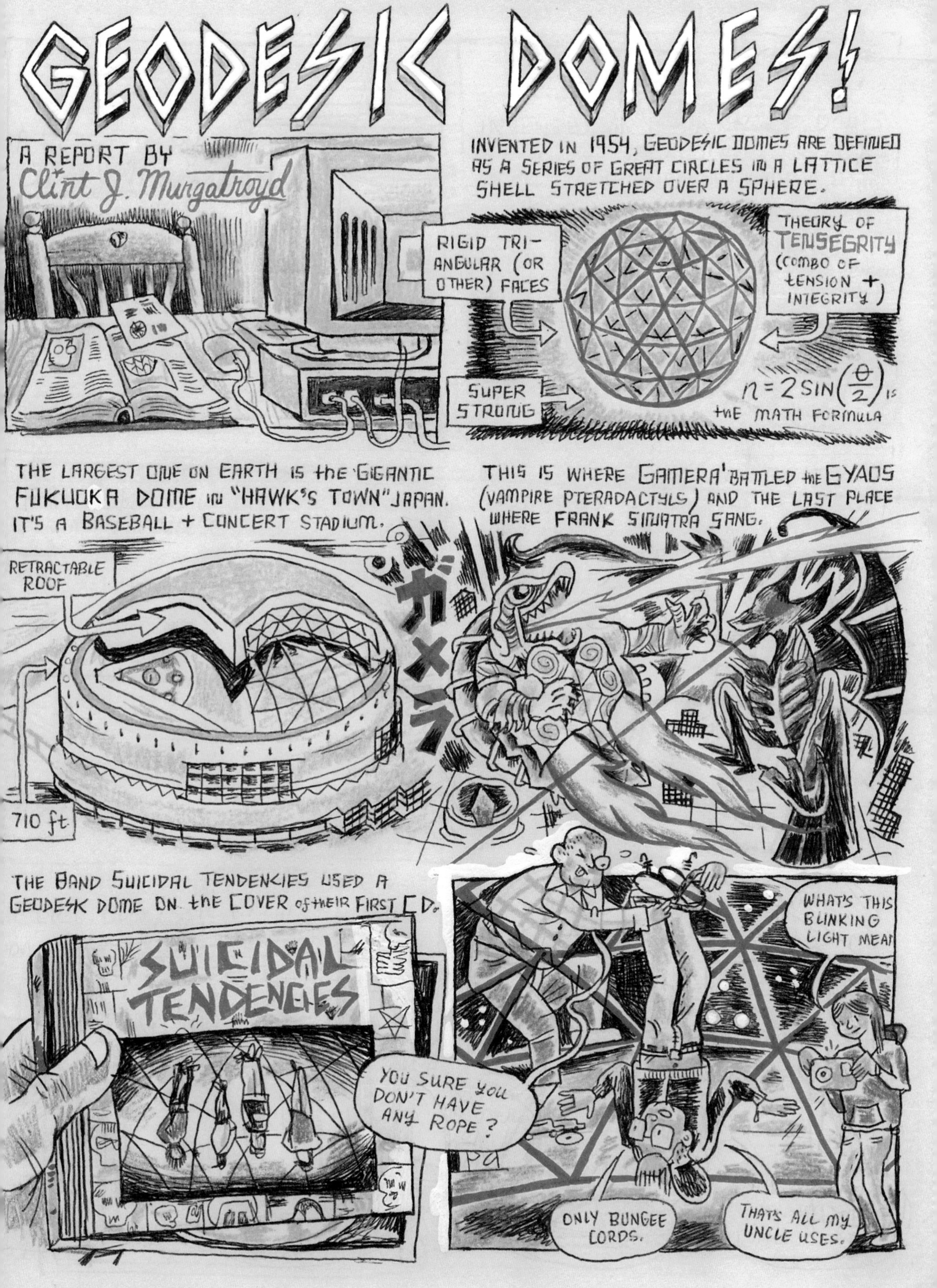
GEODESIC DOMES!
A REPORT BY
Clint J. Murgatroyd
INVENTED IN 1954, GEODESIC DOMES ARE DEFINED AS A SERIES OF GREAT CIRCLES IN A LATTICE SHELL STRETCHED OVER A SPHERE.
RIGID TRIANGULAR (OR OTHER) FACES
THEORY OF TENSEGRITY (COMBO OF TENSION + INTEGRITY)
SUPER STRONG
n = 2 SIN(θ/2) IS THE MATH FORMULA
THE LARGEST ONE ON EARTH IS THE GIGANTIC FUKUOKA DOME IN "HAWK'S TOWN" JAPAN. IT'S A BASEBALL + CONCERT STADIUM.
RETRACTABLE ROOF
710 ft.
THIS IS WHERE GAMERA BATTLED THE GYAOS (VAMPIRE PTERADACTYLS) AND THE LAST PLACE WHERE FRANK SINATRA SANG.
ガメラ
THE BAND SUICIDAL TENDENCIES USED A GEODESK DOME ON THE COVER OF THEIR FIRST CD.
SUICIDAL TENDENCIES
WHAT'S THIS BLINKING LIGHT MEAN
YOU SURE YOU DON'T HAVE ANY ROPE?
ONLY BUNGEE CORDS.
THAT'S ALL MY UNCLE USES.

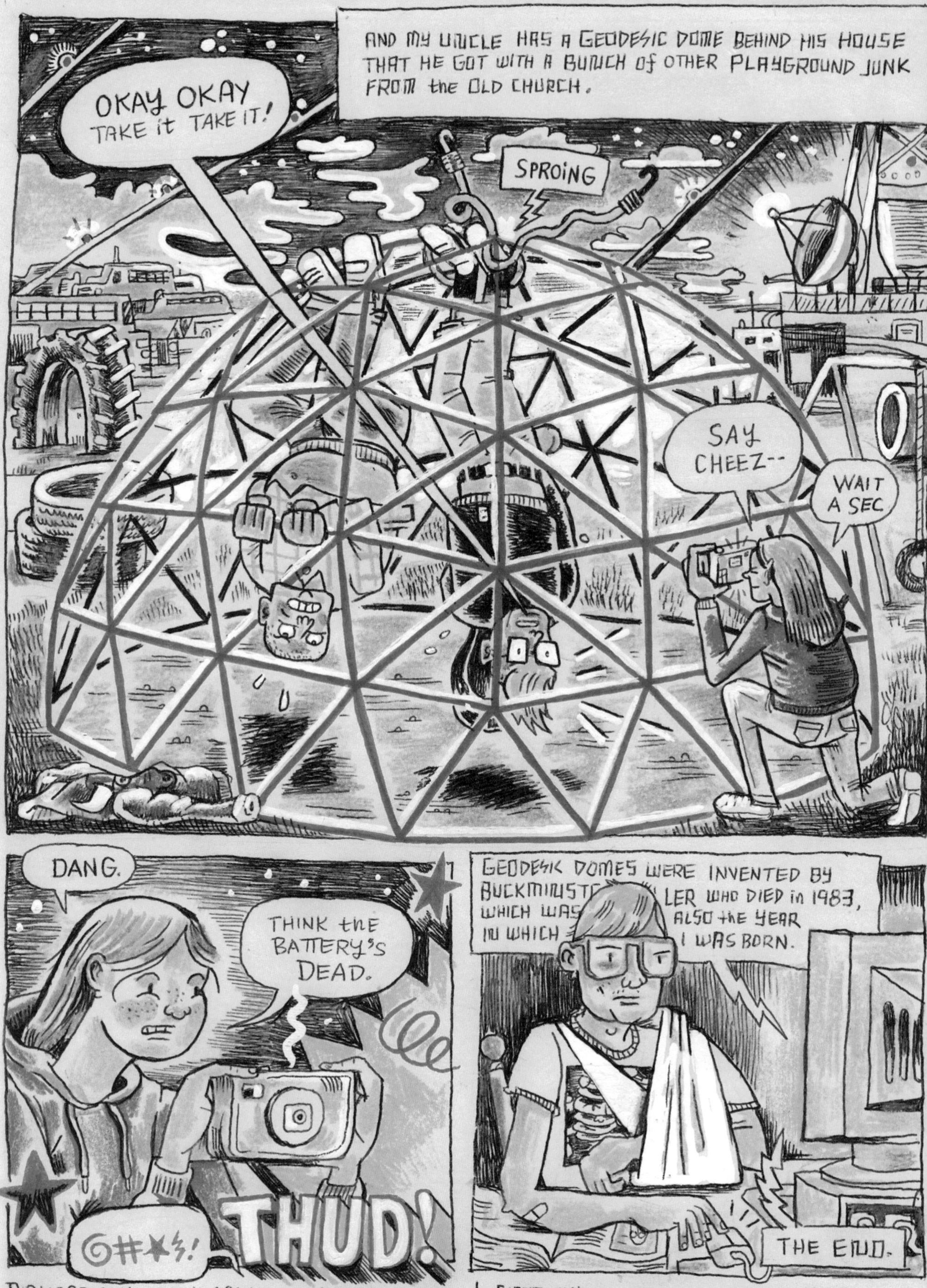
AND MY UNCLE HAS A GEODESIC DOME BEHIND HIS HOUSE THAT HE GOT WITH A BUNCH OF OTHER PLAYGROUND JUNK FROM the OLD CHURCH.
OKAY OKAY TAKE it TAKE IT!
SPROING
SAY CHEEZ--
WAIT A SEC
DANG.
THINK the BATTERY'S DEAD.
@#*$!
THUD!
GEODESIC DOMES WERE INVENTED BY BUCKMINST LER WHO DIED in 1983, WHICH WAS ALSO the YEAR IN WHICH I WAS BORN.
THE END.

BIBLIOGRAPHY: FUNK & WAGNALL ENCYCLOPEDIA, F+G
1 GIANT FLYING PREHISTORIC TURTLE, ガメラ GUARDIAN of the UNIVERSE, 1995.

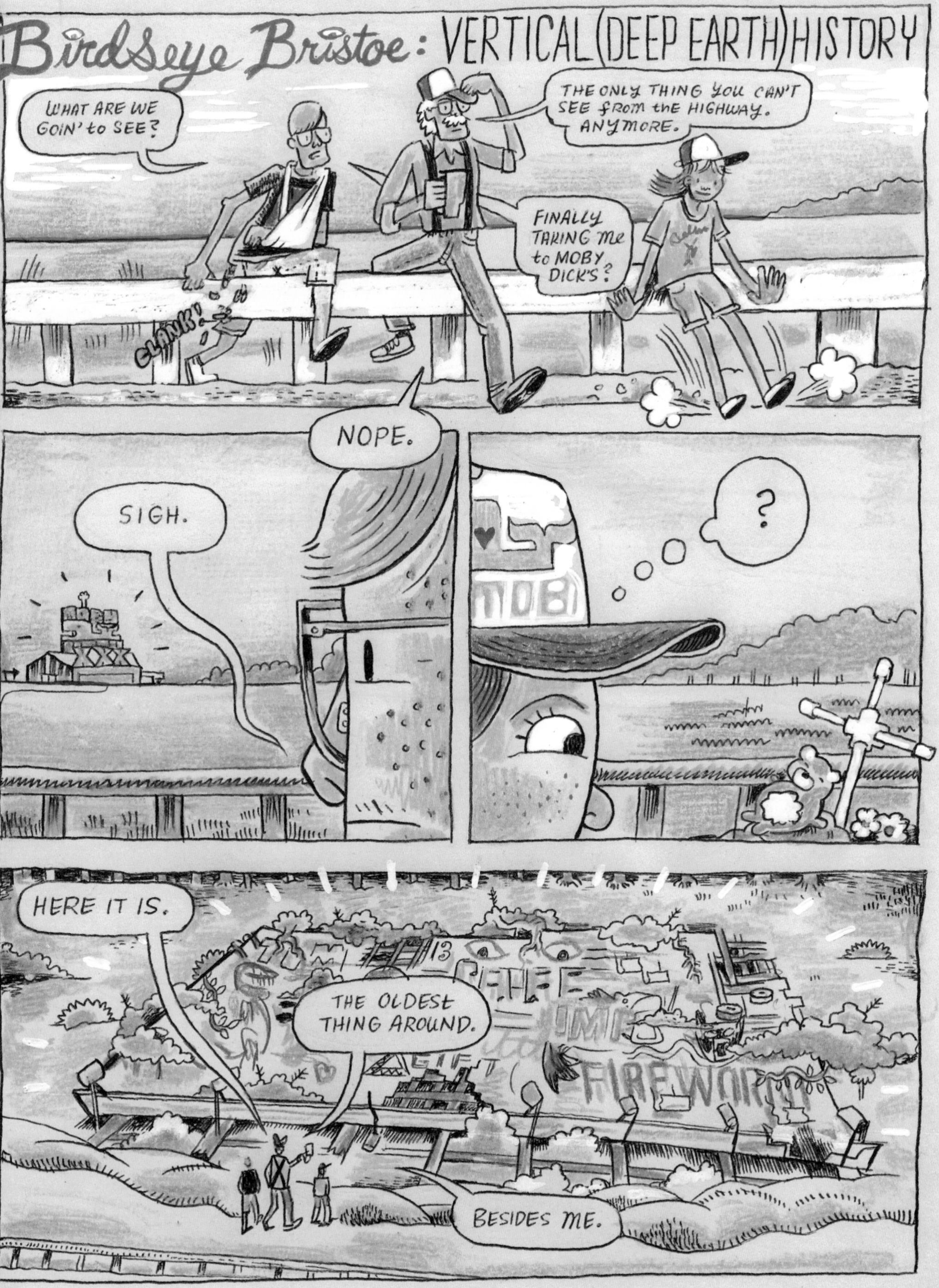
Birdseye Bristoe: VERTICAL (DEEP EARTH) HISTORY
WHAT ARE WE GOIN' to SEE?
THE ONLY THING YOU CAN'T SEE FROM THE HIGHWAY. ANYMORE.
FINALLY TAKING ME to MOBY DICK'S?
CLANK!
NOPE.
SIGH.
?
HERE IT IS.
THE OLDEST THING AROUND.
BESIDES ME.

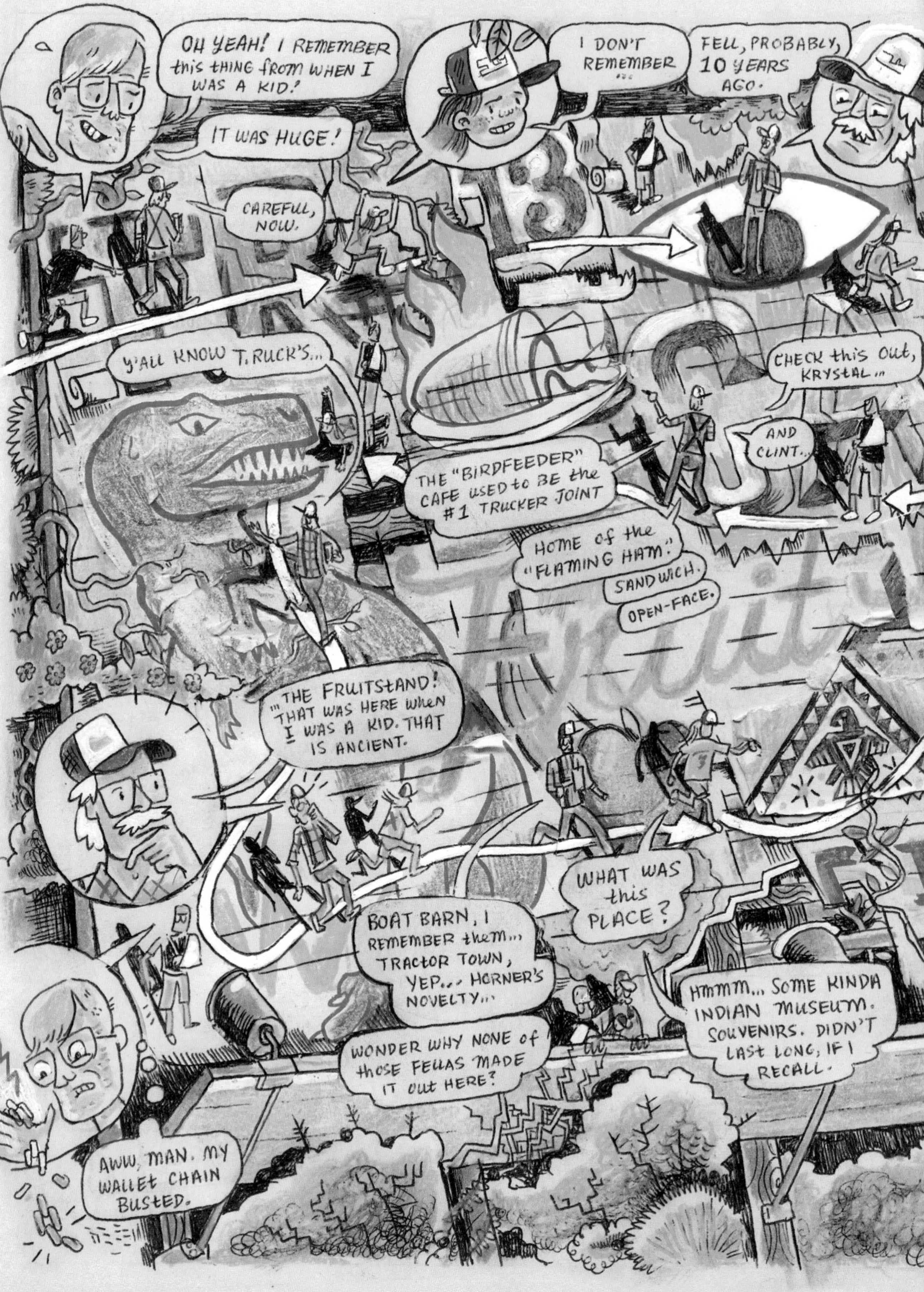
OH YEAH! I REMEMBER this thing from when I was a kid!
IT WAS HUGE!
I DON'T REMEMBER...
FELL, PROBABLY, 10 YEARS AGO.
CAREFUL, NOW.
Y'ALL KNOW T. RUCK'S...
CHECK this out, KRYSTAL...
AND CLINT...
THE "BIRDFEEDER" CAFE used to be the #1 TRUCKER JOINT
HOME of the "FLAMING HAM."
SANDWICH.
OPEN-FACE.
...THE FRUITSTAND! THAT WAS HERE when I WAS A KID. THAT IS ANCIENT.
WHAT WAS this PLACE?
BOAT BARN, I REMEMBER them... TRACTOR TOWN, YEP... HORNER'S NOVELTY...
HMMM... SOME KINDA INDIAN MUSEUM. SOUVENIRS. DIDN'T LAST LONG, IF I RECALL.
WONDER WHY NONE of those FELLAS MADE IT OUT HERE?
AWW, MAN. MY WALLET CHAIN BUSTED.

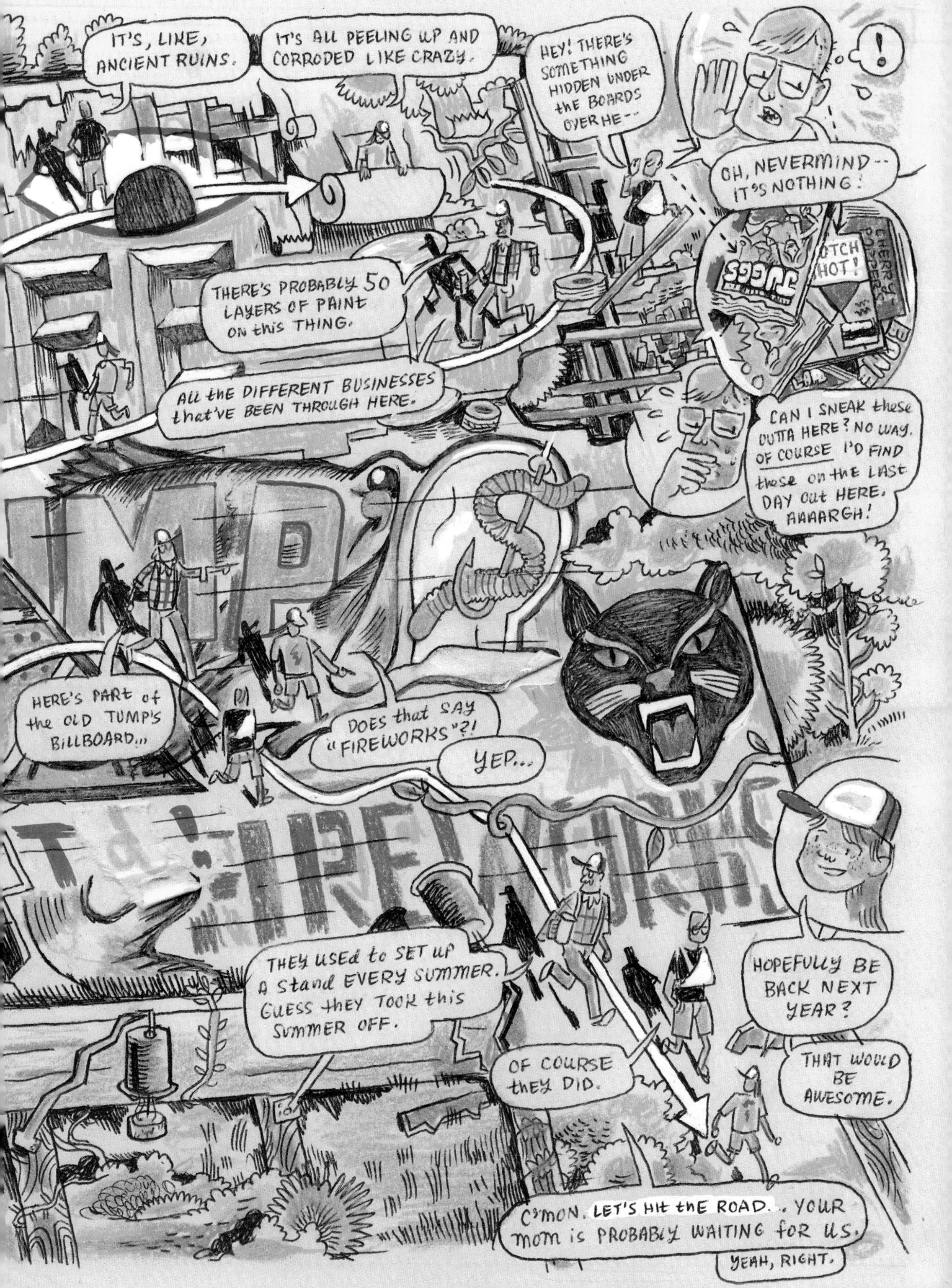
IT'S, LIKE, ANCIENT RUINS.
IT'S ALL PEELING UP AND CORRODED LIKE CRAZY.
HEY! THERE'S SOMETHING HIDDEN UNDER THE BOARDS OVER HE--
!
OH, NEVERMIND-- IT'S NOTHING!
THERE'S PROBABLY 50 LAYERS OF PAINT ON THIS THING.
ALL THE DIFFERENT BUSINESSES THAT'VE BEEN THROUGH HERE.
JUGGS
CAN I SNEAK THESE OUTTA HERE? NO WAY. OF COURSE I'D FIND THOSE ON THE LAST DAY OUT HERE. AAAARGH!
HERE'S PART OF THE OLD TUMP'S BILLBOARD...
DOES THAT SAY "FIREWORKS"?!
YEP...
THEY USED TO SET UP A STAND EVERY SUMMER. GUESS THEY TOOK THIS SUMMER OFF.
OF COURSE THEY DID.
HOPEFULLY BE BACK NEXT YEAR?
THAT WOULD BE AWESOME.
C'MON. LET'S HIT THE ROAD... YOUR MOM IS PROBABLY WAITING FOR US.
YEAH, RIGHT.

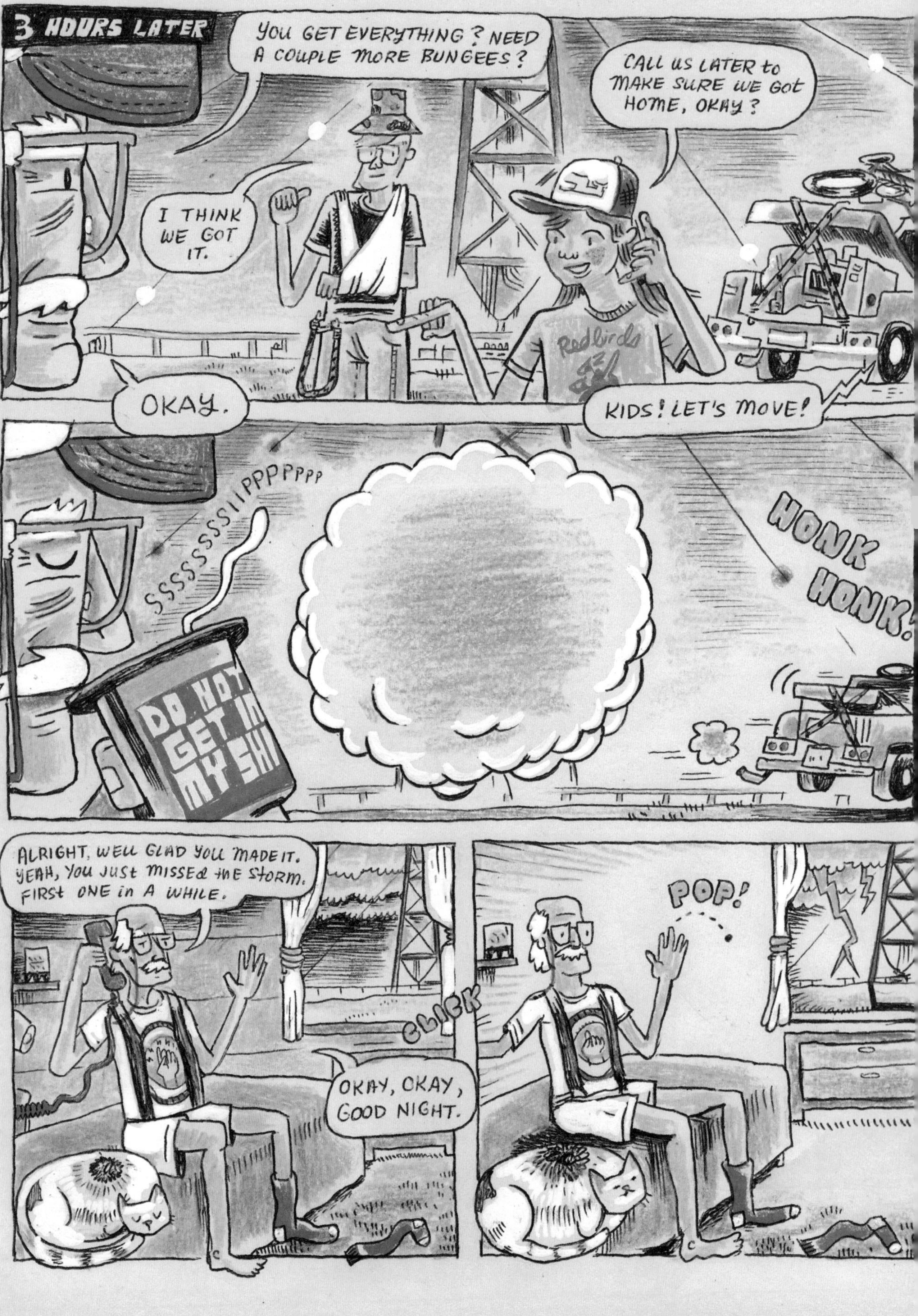
3 HOURS LATER
YOU GET EVERYTHING? NEED A COUPLE MORE BUNGEES?
I THINK WE GOT IT.
CALL US LATER to MAKE SURE WE GOT HOME, OKAY?
OKAY.
KIDS! LET'S MOVE!
SSSSSSSSIIPPPPPPP
DO NOT GET IN MY SH
HONK HONK!
ALRIGHT, WELL GLAD YOU MADE IT. YEAH, YOU JUST MISSED tHE STORM. FIRST ONE in A WHILE.
CLICK
OKAY, OKAY, GOOD NIGHT.
POP!